Book
Encyclopedia
Hull
#5
400

The Companion Guide To

Roberts'
Ultimate Encyclopedia
Of
Hull Pottery
by
Brenda Roberts

Walsworth Publishing Company
306 North Kansas Avenue
Marceline, Missouri 64658

The Companion Guide To

Roberts'
Ultimate Encyclopedia
Of
Hull Pottery

by
Brenda Roberts

Copyright 1992 © by Brenda Roberts
Library of Congress Catalog Card Number: 91-68347

Printed in the United States of America
ISBN: 0-9632136-1-X

Additional copies of this book may be ordered from:
Brenda Roberts
Highway 65 South, Route 2
Marshall, Missouri 65340

$24.95 plus $3.00 postage and handling.

Published by:
Walsworth Publishing Company
306 North Kansas Avenue
Marceline, Missouri 64658

Table Of Contents

This book is dedicated to my sons,
Jason and Justin

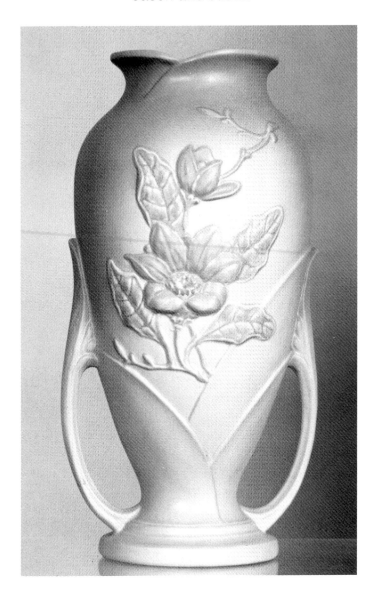

"pottery in its finest sense must have qualities of velvet-like feel to produce an emotional stir and justify a place among your finest possessions. This is a dominant characteristic. . . a balance of subdued color and style seldom obtained but always sought. See and feel the actual piece of ware to become as keenly enthused as were the inspired craftsmen."

Original Hull Promotional Materials, 1946.

About The Author

An avid American art pottery collector and dealer of general line antiques since 1974, Brenda Roberts was commissioned by Collector Books, Paducah, Kentucky, for publication of, THE COLLECTORS ENCYCLOPEDIA OF HULL POTTERY, in 1980. The continual rise of collector interest for Hull Pottery has enabled this volume, as well as its companion price guide, to be reprinted a number of times.

Since 1983, Ms. Roberts has been a member of the Advisory Board for, and a regular contributor to SCHROEDER'S ANTIQUES PRICE GUIDE, published annually by Collector Books. Ms. Roberts has also been a contributor to WALLACE-HOMESTEAD FLEA MARKET/COLLECTIBLES PRICE GUIDE and has written feature materials for publication in, THE ANTIQUE TRADER WEEKLY, THE NATIONAL JOURNAL OF GLASS, POTTERY & COLLECTIBLES, TRI-STATE TRADER, ANTIQUE WEEK, AMERICAN CLAY EXCHANGE, THE COLLECTOR, THE GLAZE, AMERICAN COLLECTOR, and THE DAZE, INC.

Ms. Roberts' continuing interest in The Hull Pottery and attention to detail, coupled with the new spirit of collector interest in American art pottery, has brought about the publication, ROBERTS' ULTIMATE ENCYCLOPEDIA OF HULL POTTERY, as well as, THE COMPANION GUIDE TO ROBERTS' ULTIMATE ENCYCLOPEDIA OF HULL POTTERY, each with accompanying price guides.

Ms. Roberts has owned and operated an antiques and appraisal business in Marshall, Missouri, called COUNTRYSIDE ANTIQUES, and currently maintains a mail order antiques business of the same name. She is continuing research on American art potteries and has other research projects in progress.

About The Book

Since the introduction of Ms. Roberts' first Hull publication, THE COLLECTORS ENCYCLOPEDIA OF HULL POTTERY, the primary justification for the continuation of her Hull collection has been founded almost exclusively on the historical aspects of the company. The quest to bring together a full accounting of the history of the Hull firm has been paramount.

THE COMPANION GUIDE TO ROBERTS' ULTIMATE ENCYCLOPEDIA OF HULL POTTERY, is an illustrated chronologically prepared guide of original company brochures which identifies over 4000 Hull items, entailing Hull's earliest years of blue and white stoneware, yellowware, Zane Grey ware, white sanitary ware and semi-porcelain production, a multitude of matte pastel artware lines of the Forties, to art productions of the Fifties. Additional brochures illustrate House 'n Garden, Ridge, Heartland and Blue-Belle dinnerware lines. This companion guide will assist in the identification of many Hull items which are rarely found marked.

Although a Brief History of the Hull Pottery is contained in this volume, a complete and thorough history of the company from it's inception to demise, can be found in ROBERTS' ULTIMATE ENCYCLOPEDIA OF HULL POTTERY, the most comprehensive and authoritative work available on the subject of Hull Pottery, which includes over 4500 examples from the author's collection of pottery wares, company information, ads and original company brochure pages, as well as a descriptive listing of over two hundred lines with dates of manufacture, a separate listing of cookie jars and canisters and over eighty illustrated trademarks.

It is hoped the volumes will not only better acquaint the public of the superior excellence and predominant features of the products of the Hull Pottery, but also to coalesce the history of a respected company in a manner of which it is deserving.

Introduction

The Hull Pottery journey takes place in the small village of Crooksville, Ohio, where pottery was a way of life, the industrial existence of which gave way to the region's being named "Pottery Center of the World." Beginning in 1905, with a single plant, Hull soon advanced to a second factory in 1907, both which operated until 1930. The first years of pottery production were devoted to common stoneware and stoneware specialties. Soon afterward, semi-porcelain dinnerware lines appeared, as did artwares and decorative tile. By the 1940's, additional classic lines of pastel matte artware emerged. The 1950's were satiated by multitudes of high quality art designs which were absolutely unequalled by others, in style, content and glaze treatments. Hull's final twenty-five years of pottery production centered on casual servingware, suitable for the kitchen or patio, and the vast Imperial floristware line.

Hull's days of reign and rule of the wholesale and retail pottery market have ended ... or have they? After eighty extremely eventful and productive years, the Hull Pottery is at rest ... or is it? While the tradition of operations has ended, the memories subsist, in lovely and serviceable wares which grace today's homes. During the Company's near century of pottery production, Hull wares were known to the trade to be exceptional in quality and value. Hull's popularity then, as now, can only be termed as monumental. The lines are quite diversified, all useful and decorative.

In 1950, the disastrous flood and fire earned Hull a local audience that took notice of lines that were never again to be produced. There were those who contemplated market speculation, however, when the company was reconstructed, the ware basically remained uncollected even though the public was acutely aware that many designs and glaze formulas were lost forever.

Hull's popularity was apparent in the early 1970's, when a group of collectors ventured from better known potteries to build the massive Hull collections that exist today. Although there were people "in the know," Hull remained rather unobtrusive for nearly another decade, while it remained on dealer's lowest shelves, taking a back seat to formidable rivals. The early Hull harbingers, with powerful judgment and direction, guided, while others observed and eventually supervened, and by the late 1970's, collector interest was profound and observable throughout the United States and Canada. Currently armed with knowledge of the final closing of the plant in 1985, Hull enthusiasts are noticeably prominent in all segments of the collecting market.

There are collectors that specialize in specific art designs; items such as wall pockets, ewers, baskets, cookie jars; specific time frames such as pre or post 1950; and specific clay bodies such as stoneware, yellowware or tile; along with collectors of Hull's famous House 'n Garden dinnerwares, and more. The diversified lines of Hull Pottery offer limitless collecting potential. And, yes, there are collectors who collect everything, a phenomena which has made this publication a reality.

Brief History Of The Hull Pottery

The family-owned and operated Hull Pottery was founded by Addis Emmet Hull, Sr., whose pottery aptitude became evident in his experience as a traveling salesman for The Star Stoneware Company, later as manager of The Globe Stoneware, and finally as organizer and President of The A. E. Hull Pottery Company.

The A. E. Hull Pottery, formed in 1905, was an early success in the tiny Village of Crooksville, Ohio, and served as a formidable rival to neighboring potteries of the Ohio Valley. The Hull Pottery was so successful that it soon outgrew it's first factory, which was constructed on the north end of China Street in Crooksville. Addis Hull secured the building, operations, and equipment of The Acme Pottery for it's second plant and immediately converted production from Acme's porcelain dinnerwares to Hull's own style of porcelain products.

"We are now without question the largest manufacturers of Stoneware Specialties in the United States. We have grown from four kilns, to a capacity of ten kilns, and two decorating kilns. All the officers are natives of Perry County except Mr. Griswold, Vice President, whose home is in Boston, Mass., and all are men of practical worth in the business."

The lines Hull offered were diversified, and as the market dictated, the company soon displayed their pattern of being flexible and adaptable in redirecting operations to meet current market demands. The consistency of flexibility the company maintained during their years of production was a definite attribute which kept the company solvent years beyond those of rival companies.

Hull's initial experience was directed to the stoneware trade and early company advertising boasted them to be the "Largest Capacity in the World," in production of "High Grade Pottery Specialties, Plain and Decorated." Lines offered in both stoneware and semi-porcelain bodies included yellowware, blended ware, white sanitary cooking ware, blue banded Zane Grey, toilet ware, cereal ware, decorated kitchenware, and more. These utilitarian lines were further complimented by art pottery, jardinieres and flower pots.

Business was quite profitable, but even with that, Hull entered into a distribution campaign with The American Clay Products Company of Zanesville, Ohio, and additionally imported volumes of novelties and kitchenwares from European countries which numbered more than the entire output of both factories. Foreign wares were sold alongside Hull's domestic production for nearly eight years.

Hull's two plants and general offices were located in Crooksville, Ohio, while an Eastern office and Showroom were located in New York. The Eastern warehouse, a very necessary part of operations, was located in New Jersey. Additionally, a Chicago office was maintained and a Branch House was located in Detroit.

The demand for stoneware products was lessening, and to meet market trends, Hull converted operations in the China Street plant to tile production in 1926. Clay for tiling operations was obtained from Crooksville's Mineral Addition, and both plain and faience tile was manufactured.

Addis remained at the helm of the Hull Pottery until his death in 1930, when his eldest son, Addis E., Jr., who had been assistant manager of the pottery, took over management of the company. James Brannon Hull, another son, held the position of accountant and bookkeeper, in charge of the orders department.

The depression years had taken their toll on American businesses during the 1930's, and Hull wisely ceased importations and closed the doors of the Jersey City warehouse in 1929. Hull discontinued tiling operations in 1931, and further closed the doors of Plant No. 1 in 1933, and the New York showroom in 1935. Although there were a number of salesmen located in northern, southern and western offices, all operations were being directed from Plant No. 2, which housed newer equipment, having earlier installed the pottery's first continuous kiln at a cost of nearly $75,000.

Addis, Jr., was contemplating the pursuit of management outside the family pottery, and in 1937, accepted management of the Shawnee Pottery in Zanesville, Ohio. When confronted with the outside business venture, Hull very carefully provided for the future employment of company personnel and for the future continuous flow of production for his father's firm by accepting a long-term contract with Shulton of New York for production of pottery cosmetic and soap product containers. Hull left the company knowing it was secure, jobs and production would continue under the direction of the company's new President, Gerald Watts, governed by provisions of this contractual agreement with Shulton.

This was the first time in Hull's history to be headed by someone outside the Hull family. Watts, however, was the son of William Watts, an initial organizer of the A. E. Hull Pottery firm. The company had previously been clearly established as a giant in the field of ceramics by Addis E. Hull, Sr., and Addis E. Hull, Jr., and Watts continued to project the same strong and diversified image by the major infiltration of the fluid and lovely pastel art lines for which this pottery is most famous.

In the late 1920's, Hull, as well as many other American companies, dealt in voluminous sales of foreign imports. Now, ten-plus years into this practice, the flood that overcame the market was nearly disastrous for local manufacturers. U. S. importers of foreign wares had created their own monster. Hull was seriously in need of great numbers of designs of artwares to compete not only with local rivals, but also with their foreign competition. Times demanded American wares with a distinctively local look and feel. Necessity demanded that local manufacturers out-design, out-merchandise and out-distance all foreign competition.

America reclaimed it's retail market when the War abruptly halted any desire or demand for imported wares. The company was able to market all the artwares which could be produced, however, the War made labor and materials scarce. The redirection of raw materials into the War effort was a problem, and modelers and other experienced craftsmen were scarce.

Watts' massive movement toward art pottery was definitely positive competition for other art pottery manufacturers, and soon, vases, baskets, ewers, wall pockets, rose bowls, console bowls, along with other styles were abundant. Chain stores such as Mattingly, G. C. Murphy, F. W. Woolworth, McCrory, Federated Stores, Ben Franklin and Kresge were leaders in Hull sales. The pastel-tinted artwares of Hull, embossed with realistic floral sprays, virtually flooded the market. Soothing to the senses, and simplistic in style, the pottery's distinctive look and feel proved to be Hull's "trademark" of the Forties. The Hull Pottery had most assuredly captured the attention of a nationwide art pottery market with their creations.

The future seemed promising in all respects, until fire and flame, the potter's most impairing plague, became a reality on June 16, 1950. A four-hour downpour that day changed Hull history. In the Village of Crooksville, water ran seven feet deep on Main Street and stood four feet deep inside the Hull plant. When covered by water, the fiery pottery kiln of the Hull Company exploded, setting the plant ablaze. The deep waters kept most firemen from being able to get near enough to fight the fire, and the few firemen able to reach the scene stood by helplessly without equipment. The firemen, as well as local townspeople and employees of the pottery were forced to stand by and watch the pottery burn.

By dawn, it was certain that the Hull Pottery was no more than a rubble of smoke and ashes. In a matter of a few hours, earth's elements had rendered the pottery totally useless. The kiln had exploded, the roof was gone and fire had razed the entire plant. All that remained were structural walls and charred waste within.

Potteries were typically plagued by fires, they were a fact of life to workers in this industry. Few burned-out potteries survived, but fewer had the dynamic forces that Hull was afforded. The people behind this pottery proved to all that they were survivors and this company would rise from the ashes. James Brannon Hull was elected new President and served as the dynamic force behind the reconstruction.

New bodies were formulated, new wares were available to the market by late 1951, and by January 1, 1952, the company was fully restored and officially reopened as The Hull Pottery Company. Hull's new plant was built for in-line pottery production with only the latest and most modern equipment installed.

Production lines of the Fifties proved to be very crisp, innovative, striking examples of artware. Louise E. Bauer, headed up the modeling department and new and different designs each year cultivated profitable sales for the company. Although artwares dominated the sales picture for the years of the Fifties, Hull continued to manufacture down-to-earth utilitarian kitchenware lines, which too, emerged in redesigned shapes and updated glazes. With kitchenwares remaining on the market alongside Hull's art designs, the company remained in a position that pleased not only the retail buyer of artware, but also the customer needing to stock their shelves with utility lines and kitchenwares.

In the late 1950's, the company procured a new and demanding market by having previously interspersed plain, yet sophisticated lines with their art designs. These items were soon discovered by the florist trade to be economical proven sellers and the Floristware market was fully established by Hull in 1960.

At this same time, J. B. Hull, having tremendous insight into current market trends, convinced Board Members to make major changes in production in order to keep their firm economic market stance. The California movement toward casual living in nearly every aspect of daily living, prompted Hull to make an abrupt change from artware to dinnerware. Hull's leadership was sure and steady, and adaptable to change, and so began the twenty-five year success story of House 'n Garden ovenproof casual servingware.

James Brannon Hull remained President of the Hull Pottery until his death in 1978, when management shifted to the hands of Henry Sulens. Now, for the second time in Hull history, management was at the disposal of an outsider. Sulens was not a pottery man, nor was he from the Ohio pottery region. Change was difficult and management and personnel had many disputes. The Hull Pottery was losing ground with solid repeat customers and major contracts were lost due to labor strikes and lapses in production.

Management replaced Sulens on May 26, 1981, with Larry Taylor. The disturbances within the plant continued and affected not only output, which should have been close to 50,000 pieces per day, but also the final outcome of the plant itself. Taylor, also an outsider to pottery production, set forth to build on the solid reputation and respect Hull had earned from past years as a major supplier of quality dinnerware and floristware. What Taylor failed to realize was, at that time, the Hull Pottery was enmeshed in problems that were far beyond his ability to solve.

Although there were new dinnerware styles, there were also major differences of opinion which kept the company from moving ahead. Equipment replacements were needed, the kiln was too large, and operating costs too great to provide a profitable year-end picture for the smaller numbers of wares being produced at that time. Operational costs

11

to fire the kiln were in excess of $10,000 per month, and it was estimated that in order to justify it's operation, three million dollars in sales per year were necessary. Hull had not produced that sales volume since the early 1970's. Decisions for changes were left unmade, and Hull struggled with current equipment and operations.

A major problem which surfaced during the early 1980's, included a letter from the Environmental Protection Agency instructing the company to clean up lead wastes in and around the plant. The letter, delivered in April, 1981, remained unnoticed for nearly a year. If EPA's letter regarding the new legislation for the clean up had been adhered to in a timely manner, all could have been saved, Hull would have been afforded the same time period for waste clean up as other potteries. Regardless of management transition, and Taylor's good intentions to make up for lost time, the government considered the pottery's delay in clean up action as a blatant refusal to adhere to law. Continuing problems with the EPA ultimately resulted in Federal Court litigation and funding needed for the clean up was met through operations money of the pottery plant.

After having pioneered the early uncertain years with numerous area competitors of the pottery trade, the uncertainty of the depression years, reduced output and decreased materials necessary for the War effort, disastrous ends by flood and fire, conflicts over reconstruction of the plant, shakey stability due to loss of family leaders within the company's structural foundation, numerous employee layoffs and strikes, and monumental problems with the Environmental Protection Agency, the Hull Company could withstand no more. The doors of the Hull Pottery were closed August 6th, 1985, during it's eighth employee strike.

Whether it was a case of a company and it's officials too weary to fight any longer or just plain economics, a tired old company closed it's doors. The walls within, as well as the townspeople in the small Village of Crooksville, Ohio, continued to hope for a miracle, believing this was not a fitting end to the pottery tradition, or the area craftsmen which had made the Hull a showplace in the "Pottery Center of the World," since 1905.

With little or no dignity, the Pottery died a slow death. A pottery plant with no production in sight, seemingly worthless to Stockholders and Board Members, set plans in motion by President, Larry Taylor, to have the pottery dismantled piece by historical piece. The building's interior was sold for salvage, including the bricks of the great tunnel kiln. The razed Hull building was sold to Terrance Zahn, owner of the Friendship Potteries of Roseville, Ohio.

All that remains of the Hull Pottery is a corporation name, a trademark which has had it's price, a three-man Board of Directors consisting of Larry Taylor, Marlin King, and Jack Frame and a small portion of real estate divided from the plant by the railroad, the site formerly used to dispose of Hull's contaminated lead wastes.

NO. 18 BOWL

We also put this up in our No. 44 piece Sets, from 5 in. to 10 in. inclusive, each set wrapped nicely, at $1.35 per set.

F. O. B. FACTORY. NO PACKAGE CHARGE.

13

No. 25—7-piece Bowl or Nappy Set. Decorated in blue underglaze bands with gold lines. Can be used to bake in as well as to serve in. Are easily cleaned. Each set nicely wrapped, $1.65. Set consists of:

1—4-in., Actual Size .... 4⅝ in.
1—5-in., Actual Size .... 5¼ in.
1—6-in., Actual Size .... 6¼ in.
1—7-in., Actual Size .... 7¼ in.
1—8-in., Actual Size .... 8½ in.
1—9-in., Actual Size .... 9⅝ in.
1—10-in., Actual Size .... 10⅝ in.
Our No. 40—6-Pce. Set same as No. 25 without the 10-in. Nappy .... $1.20 Ea.
Our No. 23—7 Pce. Set same as No. 25 without Gold lines .... $1.35 Ea.

No. 20, 7-Pce. Bowl or Nappy Set. Decorated in yellow underglaze with Gold lines. For baking and serving. Can be used for Salads, Fruits, or as Mixing Bowls. An ornament to any table. From 4-in. to 10-in. inclusive. Each set nicely wrapped, $1.65 Our No. 20. 6-Pce. Set, same as No. 20 exclusive of 10-in. Nappy $1.50 Ea. Our No. 22, 7-Pce. Set, same as No. 20 without Gold lines $1.35 Ea.

F. O. B. FACTORY. NO PACKAGE CHARGE.

Our No. 50—10-Pce. Favorite Cooking or Casserole Set.

1—7-in. or 8-in. Casserole   1—5-in. Nappy
3—6-in. Nappy   6—4-in. Nappy
Per Set $1.50

Our No. 41—6-Pce. Nappy Set.

1—4-in. Nappy, $1.00 per doz. open stock   1—7-in. Nappy, $2.00 per doz. open stock
1—5-in. Nappy, 1.30 per doz. open stock   1—8-in. Nappy, 2.50 per doz. open stock
1—6-in. Nappy, 1.50 per doz. open stock   1—9-in. Nappy, 4.00 per doz. open stock
Per Set $1.12

Both of these sets decorated in Blue underglaze lines

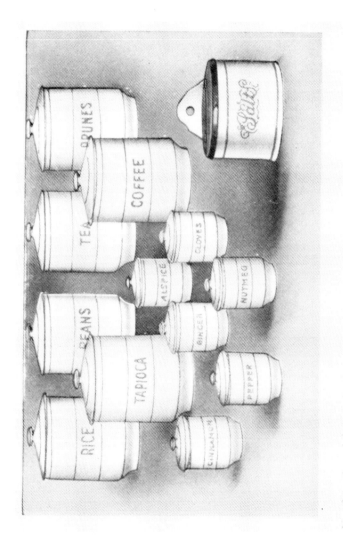

No. 10—Cereal Jar, gold lines and letters ..... $4.80 per doz.
No. 11—Spice Jar, gold lines and letters ..... 2.40 per doz.
No. 12—Salt Box, gold lines and letters ..... 7.80 per doz.
No. 8—Salt Box, black letters only ..... 3.00 per doz.
One 13 Pc. Cereal Set consists of 6 only No. 10 assorted Cereal Jars,
6 only No. 11 assorted Spice Jars and 1 only Salt Box ..... 4.00 per set.

F. O. B. FACTORY. NO PACKAGE CHARGE.

17

No. 2—2 gal. Water Jar .... $2.50 each
No. 3—3 gal. Water Jar .... 2.50 each
No. 4—4 gal. Water Jar .... 3.50 each
    Faucets, $1.00 each.
    Utility Jars are lettered Flour, Bread, Cakes, Lard, Sugar, etc., and are made in following sizes:
2-qt. Utility Jar .... $1.00 each   8-qt. Utility Jar .... $1.80 each
4-qt. Utility Jar .... 1.20 each   12-qt. Utility Jar .... 2.75 each
                6-qt. Utility Jar .... $1.40 each
    Any of the above pieces in Plain White without lettering can be furnished at 10% off above list.

F. O. B. FACTORY. NO PACKAGE CHARGE.

18

No. 120—15-Pce. Cereal Set.
Blue Decoration with Black Lettering
$8.20 Per Set.

No. 123—15-Pce. Cereal Set.
Delft Scene and Black Lettering
$6.50 Per Set.

We also make

No. 119—15-Pce. Set, Grecian Border, Blue, Top and Bottom $6.00 each
No. 121—15-Pce. Set, Grecian Border, Gold, Top and Bottom.   6.50 each
No. 122—15-Pce. Set, Conventional Decal, Top only   8.50 each
No. 124—15-Pce. Set, Conventional Decal, Top only   5.40 each
No. 128—15-Pce. Set, Decalcomania, Top and Bottom   6.20 each

No. 11—Cereal Set, 12 Pieces.
Decorated in Blue Lines and Black Letters.
Per Set $3.50

No. 23
7-Pce. Blue Band Nappy Set.

1 — 4-in.
1 — 5-in.
1 — 6-in.
1 — 7-in.　Per Set $1.38
1 — 8-in.
1 — 9-in.
1 — 10-in.

No. 30
Blue Band Hotel Cuspidor

No. 99
Blue Band Parlor Cuspidor

No. 99—Blue Band Cuspidor .... $4.50 doz
No. 25—Brown Band Cuspidor .... 4.50 doz
No. 28—Green Band Cuspidor .... 4.50 doz
No. 26—Green Band Cuspidor, Hotel shape .. 4.50 doz
No. 27—Brown Band Cuspidor, Hotel shape .. 4.50 doz

No. 6 Jug.
Underglaze Blue Band and Lines
42's—1   pt. .... $1.80 doz.
36's—1½ pt. .... 2.40 doz.

No. 1 Custard.......40c doz.
No. 2 Custard.......50c doz.
No. 3 Custard.......60c doz.

6's 5-lb. Banded.......$4.50 doz.
9's 3-lb. Banded....... 3.20 doz.
12's 2-lb. Banded....... 2.20 doz.

Yellow Embossed.
3-lb. Bld. Butter..... $3.50 doz.

36's— 5½ in.......$ .60 per doz.
30's— 6½ in....... .84 per doz.
24's— 7½ in....... 1.20 per doz.
18's— 8½ in....... 1.80 per doz.
12's— 9¼ in....... 2.40 per doz.
9's—10½ in....... 3.00 per doz.
6's—11½ in....... 4.50 per doz.
4's—12½ in....... 6.00 per doz.
3's—13½ in....... 9.00 per doz.
2's—14½ in.......12.00 per doz.
1's—15½ in.......18.00 per doz.

6's Yellow Open, 9 -in.....$3.25
9's Yellow Open, 8 -in..... 2.50
12's Yellow Open, 7½-in..... 1.70

5-Pt. Y. Dairy Jug.
$30.00 gross.

Our No. 1—6-Pce. Yellow Bowl Set consists of—

1—5-in., actual size	5⅜ in.	1— 8-in., actual size	8½ in.
1—6-in., actual size	6⅜ in.	1— 9-in., actual size	9½ in.
1—7-in., actual size	7⅜ in.	1—10-in., actual size	10½ in.

Each Set 66 2-3c.

F. O. B. FACTORY. NO PACKAGE CHARGE.

Mottled Flue Band and Plain White Bowls

5-in	$ .60
6-in	.72
7-in	.90
8-in	1.20
9-in	1.60
10-in	2.00
11-in	2.60
12-in	3.60

White Combinets $ .60
B. B. or Tint   .50

White Chamber
9's White open $30.00 gross
9's White covered   45.00 gross
12's White open   25.50 gross
12's White covered   37.80 gross

Soap Slab
$1.50 dozen

5-in	Tint	$ .60
6-in	Tint	.72
7-in	Tint	.90
8-in	Tint	1.20
9-in	Tint	1.60
10-in	Tint	2.00
11-in	Tint	2.60

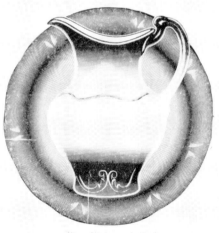

Rex Ewer and Basin

9's	White	$12.00 doz
12's	White	8.00 doz
9's	Tinted	12.50 doz
12's	Tinted	8.50 doz

Embossed E. & B.

9's	White	$12.00
9's	Tinted	12.50
12's	White	8.00
12's	Tinted	8.50

5-Pt. Plum Dairy Jug.
$24.00 gross

Hall Box Jug—3 Pints
$19.20 gross

8-in. Bird Tankard, Blue Tint
$21.00 gross

SANITARY
WATER KEG

Front View
Rear View Another Design
3-gal., each .... $ .72
4-gal., each 96
5-gal., each 1.20
6-gal., each 1.44
    Faucets, $1.00.

No. 20—7½-in. Cuspidor.
$20.00 gross

7½-in. Mottled Cuspidor
$20.00 gross

7½ Tall Tint
$22.50 gross

Embossed Open Chambers.
9's Open .... $30.00 gross
12's Open .... 25.20 gross
    Add ½ for Covers.

No. 10 Salt Box
$22.50 gross

Covered Butter
2-lb. Covered, $16.80 gross
3-lb. Covered, 18.00 gross
5-lb. Covered, 24.00 gross

Lb.   Gross.
1 Open Butter   7.50
2 Open Butter   9.60
3 Open Butter 12.00
5 Open Butter 14.40

Covered Butter, Bailed
2-lb. .... $18.00 gross
3-lb. .... 22.50 gross
5-lb. .... 30.00 gross

24

Dairy Jug—5 Pint
Brown and White Lining
$24.00 gross.

Height 8 inches
Brown and White Lining
$21.00 gross.

Cherry Jug.
Brown and White Lining
$21.60 gross.

Bird Jug.
Brown and White Lining
$21.00 gross.

No. 20 Cuspidor.
$20.00 gross.

Brown and White Lined
Custard or Bean Pot
No. 1 Smooth $4.80 gross
No. 2 Smooth 4.80 gross
No. 3 Smooth 6.00 gross
No. 4 Smooth 6.00 gross

Jardiniere.
   Gross
7½-in. Brown Tulip $21.60
7½-in. Ped to match 21.60

Pipkin.
Brown and White Lined.

1½	Pint	$1.20 doz.
2	Pint	1.50 doz.
3	Pint	2.00 doz.
6	Pint	3.00 doz.

Tea Pot.
Brown and White Lining

42's	$1.80 doz.
36's	2.40 doz.
30's	3.00 doz.
24's	4.00 doz.

The above is our famous Brown and White Lined Ware. Burned to a very high heat. Vitrified and cannot craze.

F. O. B. FACTORY. NO PACKAGE CHARGE.

BLENDED WARE

7½-in. Bird Jard., $2.50 doz.
9-in. Bird Jard., $4.00 doz.

8½-in. Berry Jard., $2.80 doz.

Pint 12 x 7½ Lip Jug,
$24.00 gross

3 pint Blended Lip Jug,
$24.00 gross

8½-in. Harp Jard., $2.50 doz.

7-in. Flared Cuspido.
$4.00 gross

8½-in. Beauty Jard., $2.50 doz.

6-in. Blended Bird Jug,
$5.00 doz.

4½-in. Tan Cuspido.
$24.00 gross

Meat Tub
Sizes
15 gallons
20 gallons
25 gallons
30 gallons

Shoulder Judes
½ gallon
1 gallon
2 gallon
3 gallon
4 gallon
5 gallon

Churns
2 gallon
3 gallon
4 gallon
5 gallon
6 gallon

Black and White Butters
¼ gallon
½ gallon
1 gallon
2 gallon
3 gallon
4 gallon
5 gallon
6 gallon

Low Butter
Black and White
½ gallon
1 gallon

Press Jar
½ gallon
1 gallon
1½ gallon
2 gallon
4 gallon

Bean Pot
1 quart
2 quart
3 quart
4 quart

Milk Pans
Flat or Round Bottom
Black or White
½ gallon
1 gallon
2 gallon

French Pot
Sizes
½ gallon
1 gallon

No. 18—Blue Band Bowl

28

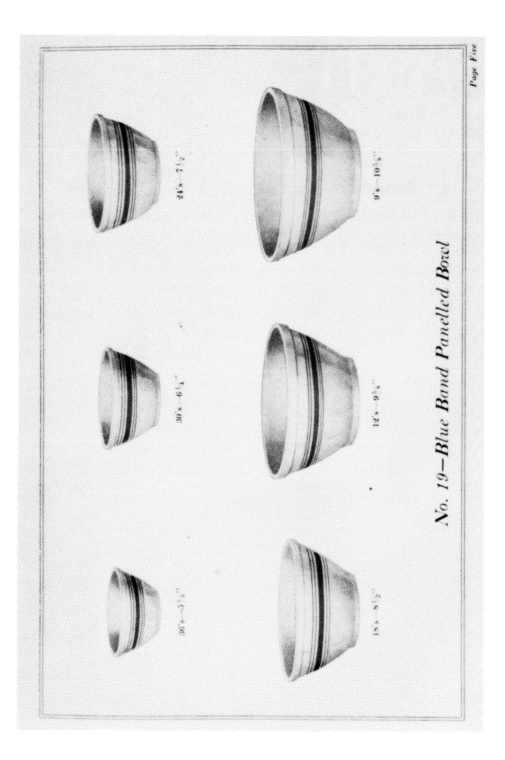

No. 19—Blue Band Panelled Bowl

29

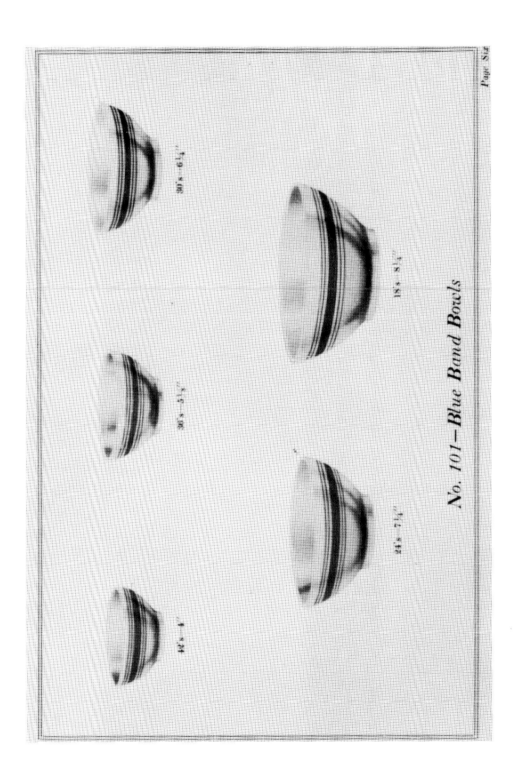

No. 101—Blue Band Bowls

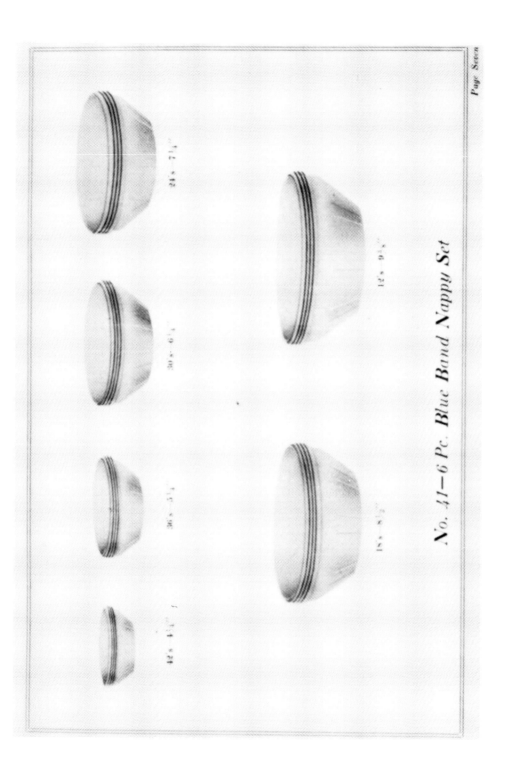

No. 41—6 Pc. Blue Band Nappy Set

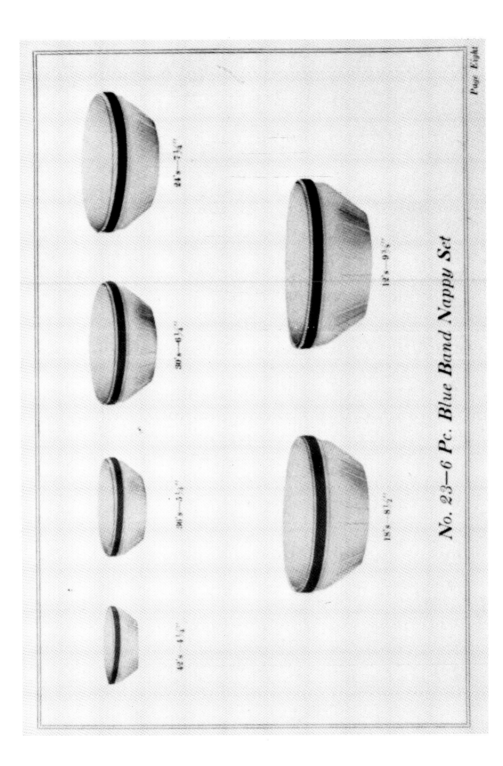

No. 23—6 Pc. Blue Band Nappy Set

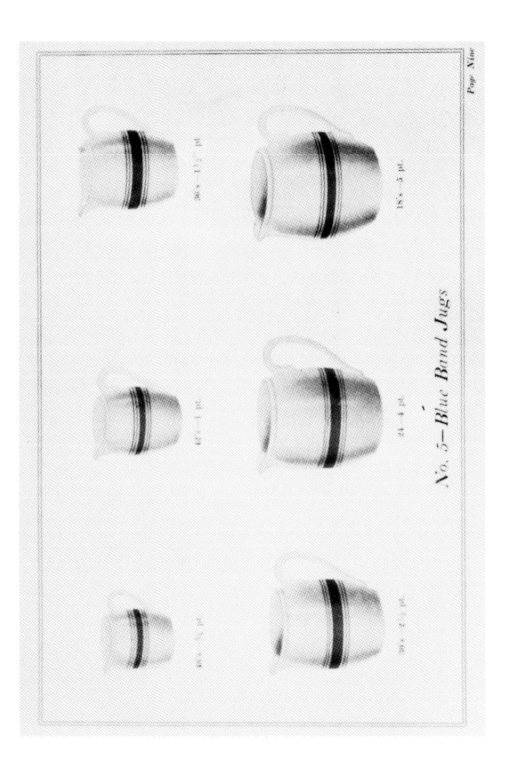

No. 5—Blue Band Jugs

4 lb. 7⅜"

3 lb. 7¼"

2 lb. 6½"

No. 7—Blue Band Butters

No. 2

No. 1

No. 4—Blue Band Custards

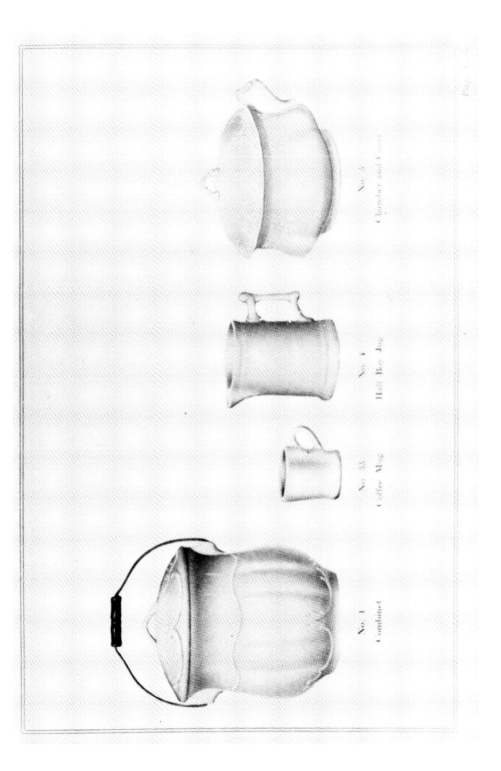

No. 2
Chamber and Cover

No. 4
Half Bag Jug

No. 35
Coffee Mug

No. 1
Combinet

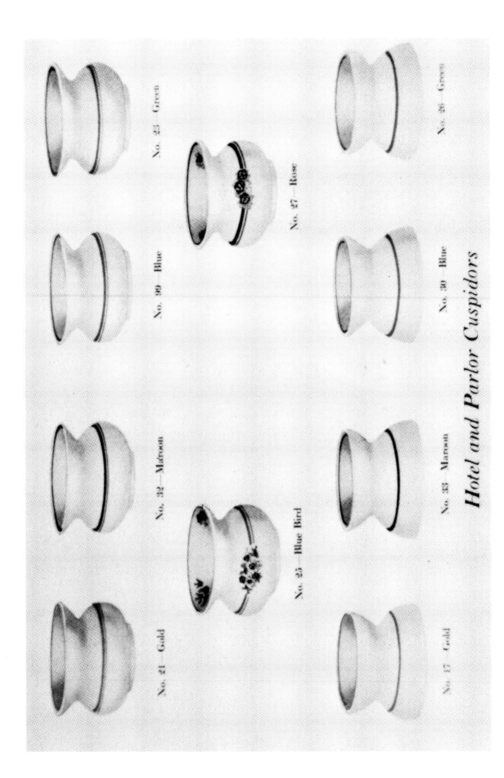

No. 25 – Green

No. 27 – Rose

No. 26 – Green

No. 99 – Blue

No. 30 – Blue

No. 32 – Maroon

No. 33 – Maroon

No. 25 – Blue Bird

No. 21 – Gold

No. 17 – Gold

Hotel and Parlor Cuspidors

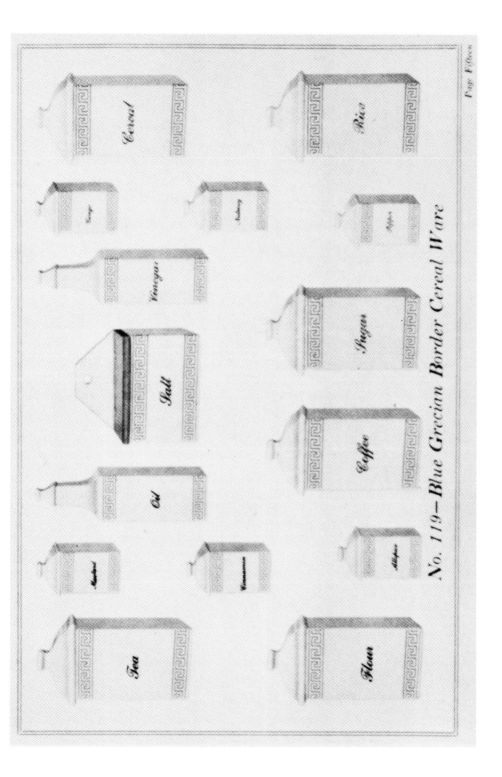

No. 119—Blue Grecian Border Cereal Ware

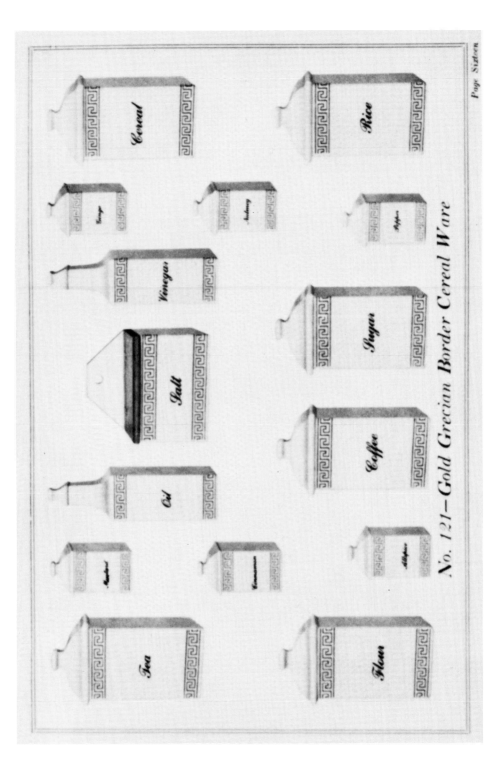

No. 121—Gold Grecian Border Cereal Ware

No. 131—Blue Double Border Conventional Vine Cereal Ware

Cereal Rice Sugar Barley Apes Vinegar Sugar Salt Coffee Oil Mustard Cinnamon Allspice Tea Flour

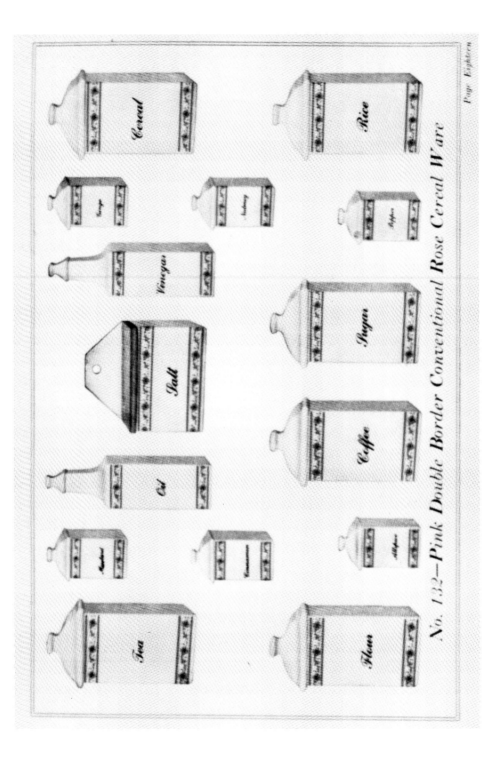

No. 132—Pink Double Border Conventional Rose Cereal Ware

No. 133—Yellow Double Border Conventional Tile Cereal Ware

41

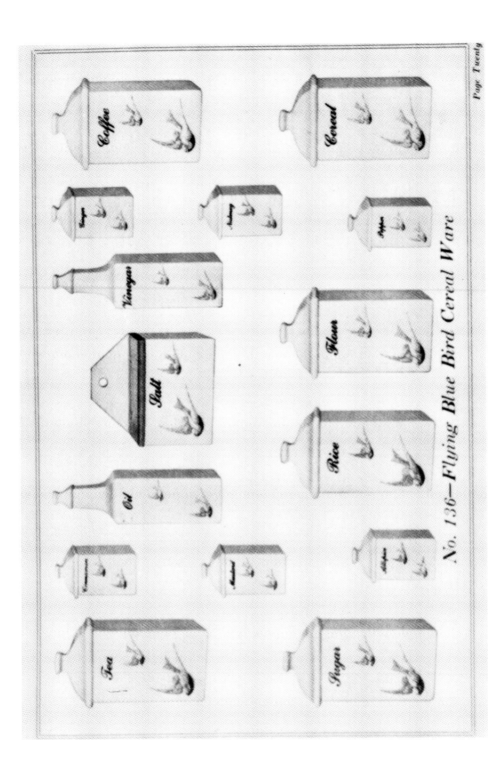

No. 136—Flying Blue Bird Cereal Ware

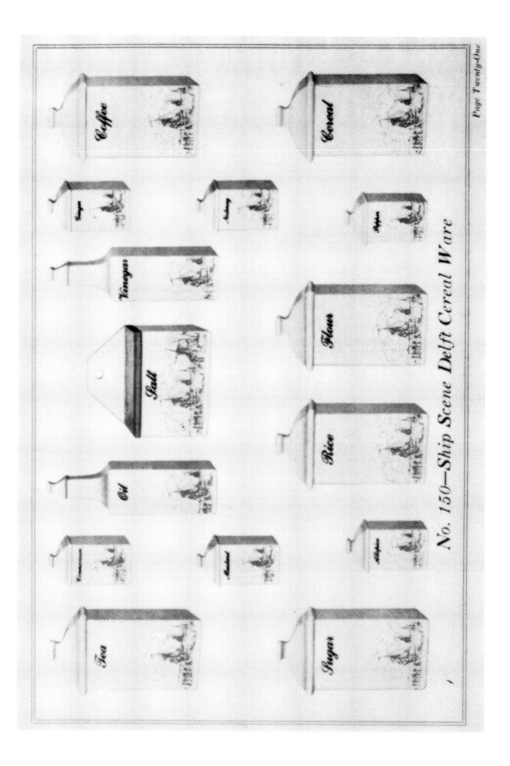

No. 150—Ship Scene Delft Cereal Ware

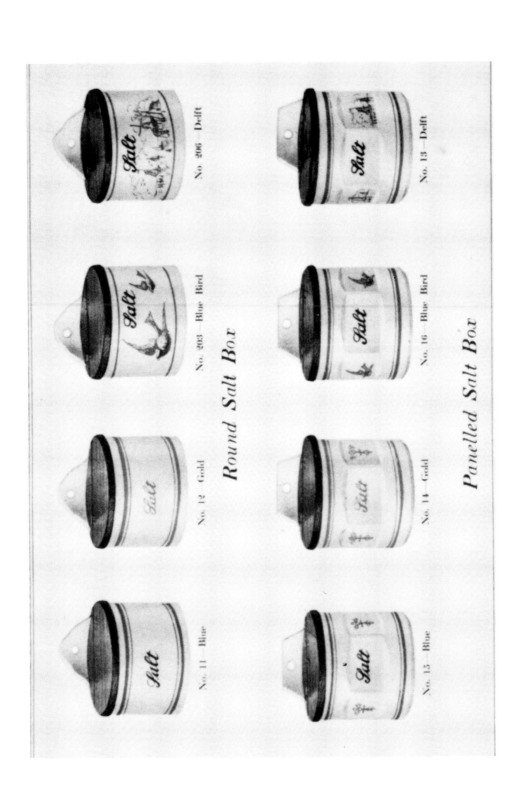

No. 206 — Delft

No. 203 — Blue Bird

No. 12 — Gold

No. 11 — Blue

Round Salt Box

No. 13 — Delft

No. 16 — Blue Bird

No. 14 — Gold

No. 15 — Blue

Panelled Salt Box

Yellow Bowls

45

No. 400—Zane Grey Jars

6 Gal

5 Gal

4 Gal

No. 400—Zane Grey Jars

No. 420—Zane Grey Bowls

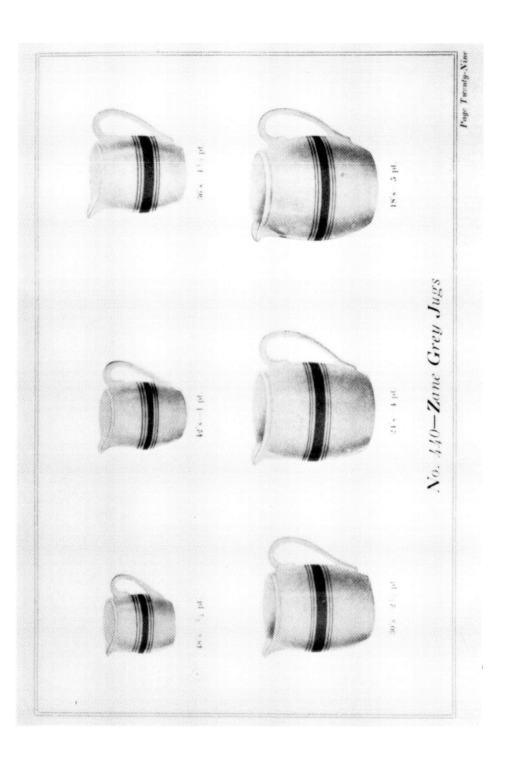

No. 440—Zane Grey Jugs

49

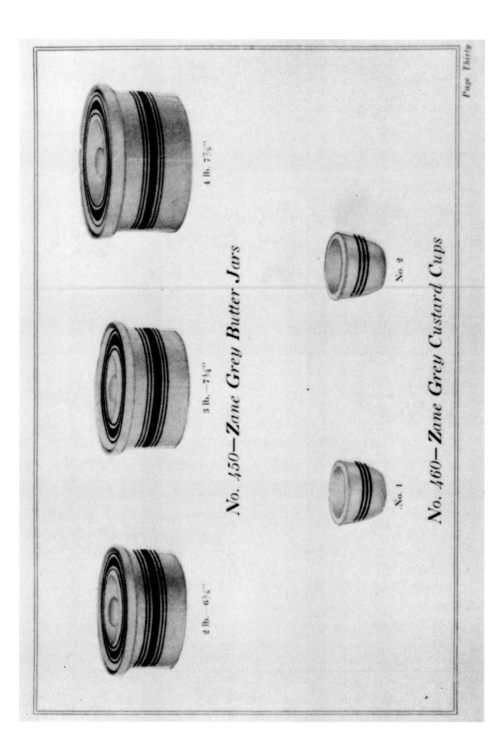

No. 450—Zane Grey Butter Jars

No. 460—Zane Grey Custard Cups

50

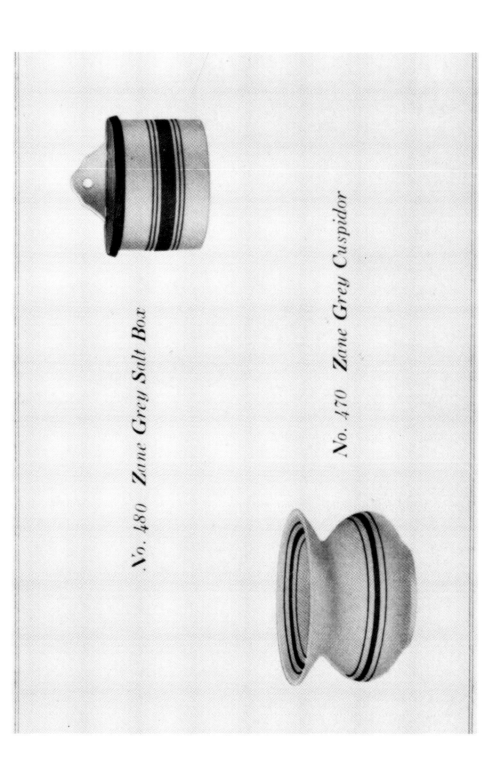

No. 480 Zane Grey Salt Box

No. 470 Zane Grey Cuspidor

LEADER COOKING ASSORTMENT

Price

95c

Per Set

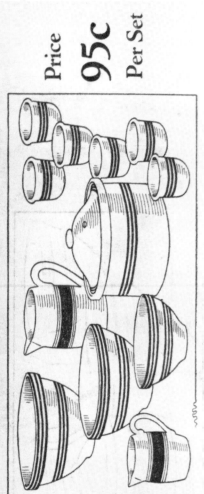

COMPOSITION

1—No. 423, 7″ Bowl.

1—No. 423, 9″ Bowl.

1—No. 423, 5″ Bowl.

1—No. 440, 30s Jug.

1—No. 440, 42s Jug.

1—No. 453, 7″ Casserole.

6—No. 460/1 Custard Cups.

KITCHEN WORX TABLE ENSEMBLE

No. 300/7—¾ PT. JUG   No. 300/7—I QT. JUG

OVEN PROOF CRAZE PROOF, IVORY WHITE WITH SPRING GREEN OR ALICE BLUE DECORATION

KITCHEN ENSEMBLE
No. 300/1. BOWL
No. 300/14 CUSTARD CUPS

OVEN PROOF
COLD PROOF
IVORY WHITE
BODY AND GLAZE

DECORATION—PIMENTO RED OR NUBIAN BLACK

No. 300/A   BAKE DISH
No. 300/15   FRENCH HANDLED CASSEROLE

HEAT PROOF, COLD PROOF. IVORY WHITE BODY AND GLAZE. DECORATED WITH PIMENTO RED OR NUBIAN BLACK STRIPES.

No. 300/4—DEEP BOWLS DESIGNED FOR QUICK, FAST STIRRING EITHER MECHANICALLY OR BY HAND.

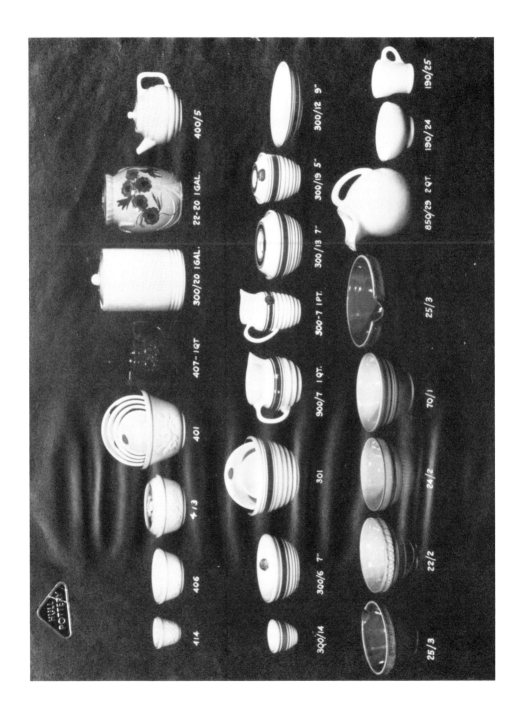

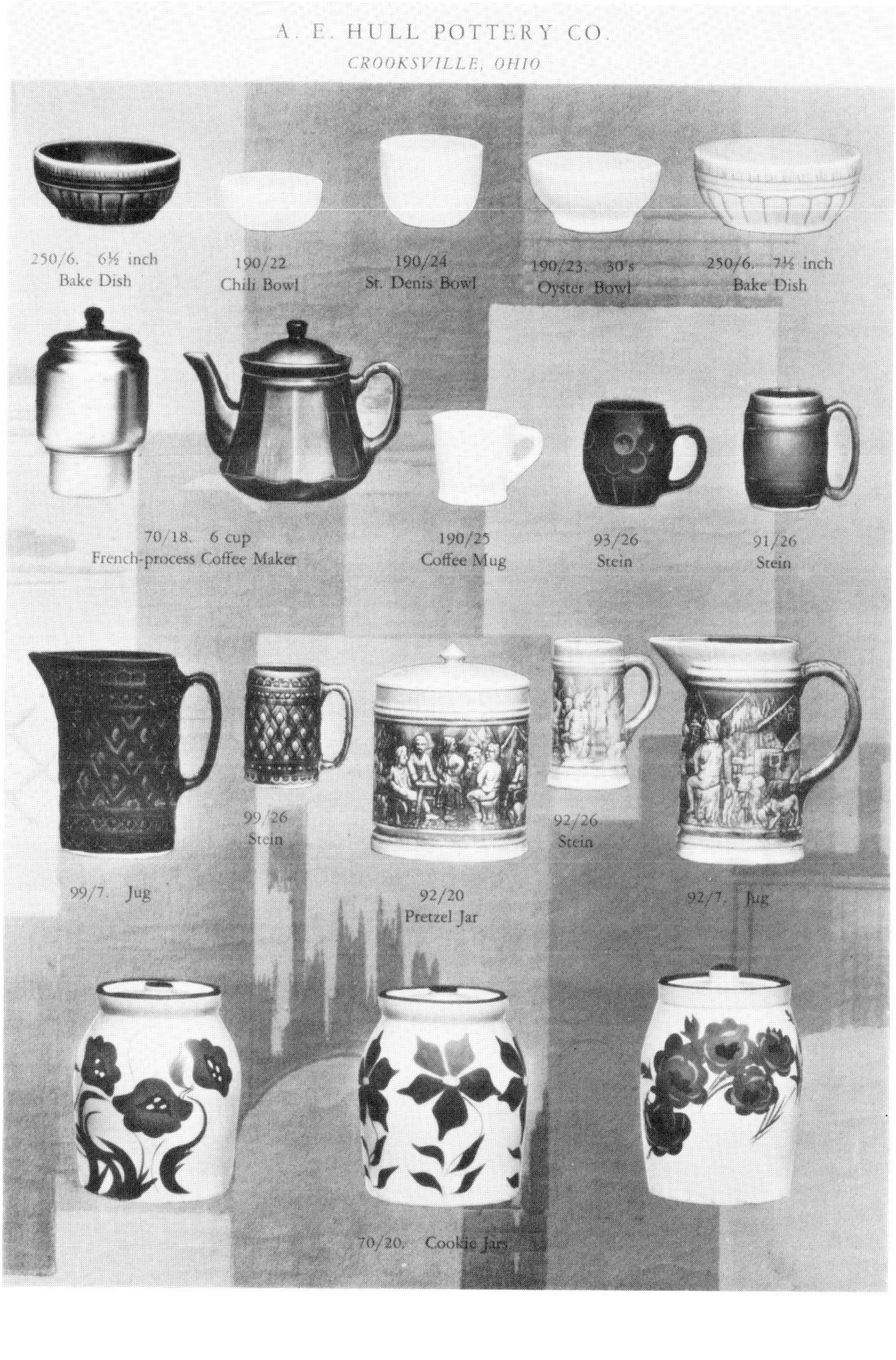
A. E. HULL POTTERY CO.
CROOKSVILLE, OHIO
250/6. 6½ inch Bake Dish
190/22 Chili Bowl
190/24 St. Denis Bowl
190/23. 30's Oyster Bowl
250/6. 7½ inch Bake Dish
70/18. 6 cup French-process Coffee Maker
190/25 Coffee Mug
93/26 Stein
91/26 Stein
99/26 Stein
92/26 Stein
99/7. Jug
92/20 Pretzel Jar
92/7. Jug
70/20. Cookie Jars

100/21. 2 lb.
Range Jar

100/14. 6 oz.
Custard Cup

100/10. 3 lb.
Refrigerator Jar

100/11. Salt Box

100/13. 7½ inch Casserole
100/16. Plate

100/7. 42's, 36's, 30's, and 24's
Jugs

100/6. 4, 5, 6, 7, 8, and 9 inch
Bake Dishes

100/1. 4, 5, 6, 7, 8, 9, 10, 11, and 12 inch
Bowls

TOP ROW
300/4 CUSTARD
300/9 JUG
300/9 RAMEKIN

SECOND ROW
300/12 PIE PLATES
300/19 FRENCH CASSE
ROLES
300/19 COVERED BEAN
POT
300/17 BAKED APPLE

THIRD ROW
300/11 BOWL SET
300/13 CASSEROLES
300/16 PLATE

BOTTOM ROW
300/6 BAKE SET
300/19 COVERED BEAN
POTS
300/4 DEEP BOWLS

OVEN PROOF, REFRIGERATOR PROOF. IVORY WHITE BODY AND GLAZE.
DECORATED WITH PIMENTO RED OR NUBIAN BLACK STRIPES.

300/15. 4½ inch
Handled Casserole

300/6. 4½ inch
Bake Dish

300/9. 4½ inch
Ramekin

300/15. 5½ inch
Handled Casserole

300/6. 5½ inch
Bake Dish

300/13. 6½ inch
Casserole

300/4. 4½ inch
Deep Bowl

300/6. 6½ inch
Bake Dish

300/13. 7½ inch Casserole
300/16. Plate

300/4. 5½ inch
Deep Bowl

300/6. 7½ inch
Bake Dish

300/13. 8¾ inch
Casserole

300/4. 6½ inch
Deep Bowl

300/6. 8½ inch
Bake Dish

300/4. 7½ inch
Deep Bowl

300/6. 9½ inch
Bake Dish

300/1. 5¼, 6¼, 7¼, 8¾
and 9¼ inch Bowl Set

62

300/12. 9 inch
Pie Plate

300/1. 5½ inch
Bowl

300/14. 6 oz.
Custard Cup

300/12. 10½ inch
Pie Plate

300/17. Baked
Apple Dish

300/1. 6½ inch
Bowl

300/19. 4½ inch
Bean Pot

300/7. 42's
Jug

300/1. 7½ inch
Bowl

300/19. 5⅛ inch
Bean Pot

300/7. 36's
Jug

300/1. 8¾ inch
Bowl

300/19. 6⅛ inch
Bean Pot

300/7. 30's
Jug

300/1. 9¾ inch
Bowl

300/19. 7½ inch
Bean Pot

36/30
Jardinier

44/31
Hanging Basket

39/35. Attached
Pot and Saucer

43/30
Jardinier

54/30
Jardinier

40/35. Attached
Pot and Saucer

51/30
Jardinier

38/34. Flower
Pot and Saucer

38/30
Jardinier

20/30
Jardinier

34/34. Flower
Pot and Saucer

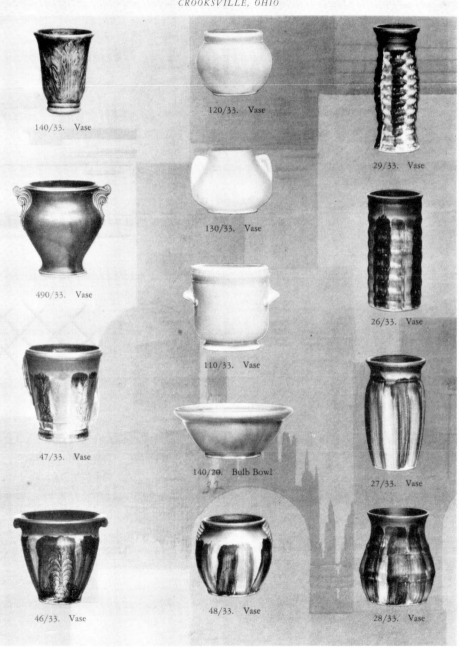

140/33. Vase

120/33. Vase

29/33. Vase

490/33. Vase

130/33. Vase

26/33. Vase

47/33. Vase

110/33. Vase

140/20. Bulb Bowl

27/33. Vase

46/33. Vase

48/33. Vase

28/33. Vase

No. 34/35 FLOWER POT AND
ATTACHED SAUCER

No. 35/35 FLOWER POT AND
SAUCER ATTACHED

No. 20/30 JARDINIER

No. 36/10 JARDINIER

THESE ITEMS ARE GLAZED IN MATT GLAZES, BERMUDA GREEN AND LOTUS BLUE.

TOP — No. 34/30/1—3½" JARDINIER, GLAZED BRIGHT EGYPTIAN GREEN
TOP RIGHT — No. 23/30—3½" JARDINIER, GLAZED MATT BERMUDA GREEN
TOP LEFT — No. 36/30—3½" JARDINIER, GLAZED MATT AUTUMN BROWN
CENTER — No. 20/30—3½" JARDINIER, GLAZED MATT OYSTER WHITE
BOTTOM LEFT — No. 83/30—3½" JARDINIER, GLAZED BRIGHT MAIZE YELLOW
BOTTOM RIGHT — No. 34/30/2—2½" JARDINIER, GLAZED MATT LOTUS BLUE
No. 30/3½" JARDINIER ASSORTMENT
6 SHAPES—6 COLORS

No. 460/33—7" VASE

No. 460/33—5½" VASE

No. 120/33—5" VASE

GLAZED IN EGG SHELL WHITE

THE "A. E. HULL" CO.
F.O.B. FACTORY—CROOKSVILLE, OHIO

MINIMUM SHIPMENT	TIME OF SHIPMENT
Minimum orders from this factory must total 100 lbs. to make an economical shipment.	Shipment will be made about 6 weeks after order is received by factory.

"A.E. HULL" POTTERY CO. Includes Pages 23 & 24 and Colored Ovenware--See Last 4 Pages.

JARDINIERE ROUND JARDINIERE HANGING BASKET POT & SAUCER VASE

NEW ARTWARE in PASTEL SHADES
AVAILABLE IN WHITE, YELLOW, TURQUOISE AND ROSE BEIGE

Domestic semi-porcelain, pure white body, asstd. pastel shades, "streamlined" embossing.

OPEN STOCK--STATE COLOR NUMBERS WANTED

1--White   2--Yellow   3--Turquoise   4--Rose beige

VASES--	Lbs Per Doz	DOZ		FLOWER POTS WITH SAUCER--	Lbs Per Doz	DOZ
57X-1171--6 in	20	1.44		57X-1181--3-3/4 in	13	1.12
57X-1172--8 in	35	2.24		57X-1182--4-3/4 in	18	1.88
57X-1173--10 in	52	3.84		57X-1183--5-1/2 in	25	2.76
57X-1174--12 in	80	5.40		57X-1184--6-1/2 in	30	3.20
				57X-1185--7-3/4 in	35	4.20
JARDINIERES--				57X-1186--8-3/4 in	60	5.40
57X-1175--3-3/8 in	8	.84		ROUND JARDINIERES--		
57X-1176--4-3/4 in	11	1.28		57X-1187--6 in	30	1.92
57X-1177--5-1/2 in	15	2.16		57X-1188--7 in	45	3.00
57X-1178--6-1/2 in	25	2.72		57X-1189--8 in	60	4.00
57X-1179--7-3/4 in	36	3.36		HANGING BASKETS--		
57X-1180--8-3/4 in	48	4.56		57X-1190--4-3/4 in	12	1.82
				57X-1191--6-1/2 in	25	3.38

5½ IN. SHRIMP PLANTERS	5 IN. SNAIL PLANTERS	5½ IN. SHELL PLANTERS	5½ IN.
57X-1192--Wt. 24 lbs per doz.	57X-1193--Wt. 18 lbs per doz.	57X-1194--Wt. 18 lbs per doz.	LADY'S HEAD PLANTERS
Doz 4.50	Doz 4.50	Doz 4.50	57X-1195--Wt. 24 lbs per doz. Doz 4.50

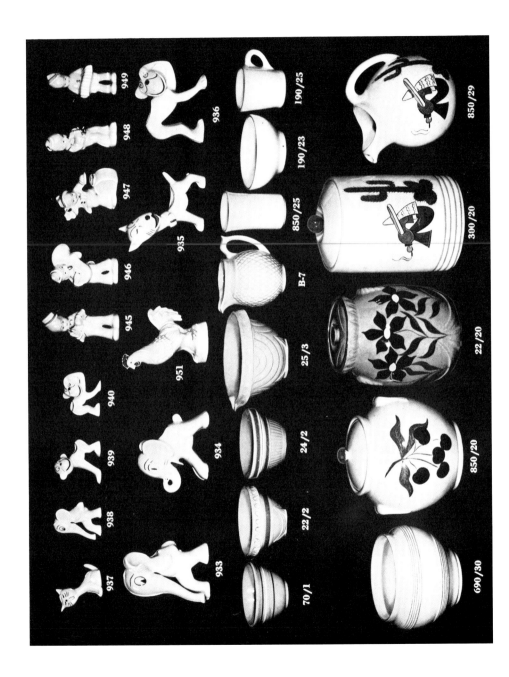

HULL'S NEW
"Sueno" LINE

With SHADED BLUE BASES
& Asstd. Pink, Blue or Cream Tops

Distinctive art ware in beautiful shapes and shadings, hand painted tulip decoration on each piece. Labeled. Attractive "Hull" display plaque FREE with order for $20.00 or more.

9 in. Vases—
57X-1203—30 lbs per doz
Doz 9.00

Vases—
57X-1200—6½ in. 16 lbs per doz.
Doz 4.80
57X-1201—8½ in. 24 lbs per doz
Doz 9.00
57X-1202—10½ in. 41 lbs per doz
Doz 12.00

Vases—Wts given per doz
57X-1209—6 in. 18 lbs
Doz 4.80
57X-1210—8 in. 27 lbs
Doz 9.00

OPEN STOCK—
STATE COLORS WANTED

1—Blue base—Pink top
2—Blue base and top
3—Blue base—Cream top

6 in. Baskets—
57X-1204—33 lbs per doz
Doz 6.00

6½ in. Vases—
57X-1205—25 lbs per doz
Doz 6.00

6 in. Vases—
57X-1206—17 lbs per doz
Doz 3.00

8 in. Vases—
57X-1207—35 lbs per doz
Doz 6.00

6½ in. Vases—
57X-1208—17 lbs per doz
Doz 4.80

6½ in. Vases—
57X-1211—20 lbs per doz
Doz 4.80

6½ in. Vases—
57X-1214—20 lbs per doz
Doz 4.80

7 in. Vases—
57X-1215—24 lbs per doz
Doz 6.00

Vases—
57X-1212—8 in. 27 lbs per doz
Doz 6.00

57X-1213—13 in. 46 lbs per doz
Doz 15.00

7 in. Jardinieres—
57X-1216—50 lbs per doz
Doz 6.00

6 in. Flower Pots with Saucer—
57X-1217—32 lbs per doz
Doz 4.80

5 in. Jardinieres—
57X-1218—15 lbs per doz
Doz 3.00

"Horn of Plenty" Vases—
57X-1219—30 lbs per doz
Doz 9.00

5½ in. Vases—
57X-1220—30 lbs per doz
Doz 3.60

5½ in. Vases—
57X-1221—30 lbs per doz
Doz 3.60

5½ in. Vases—
57X-1222—30 lbs per doz
Doz 3.60

5½ in. Vases—
57X-1223—30 lbs per doz
Doz 3.60

5½ in. Vases—
57X-1224—30 lbs per doz
Doz 3.60

24

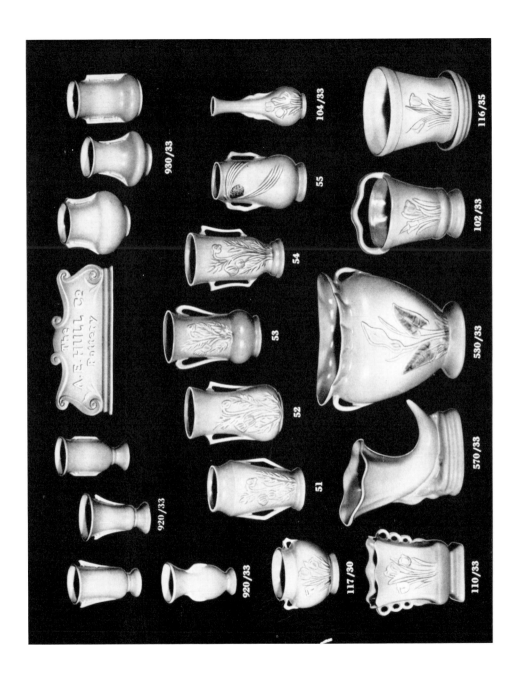

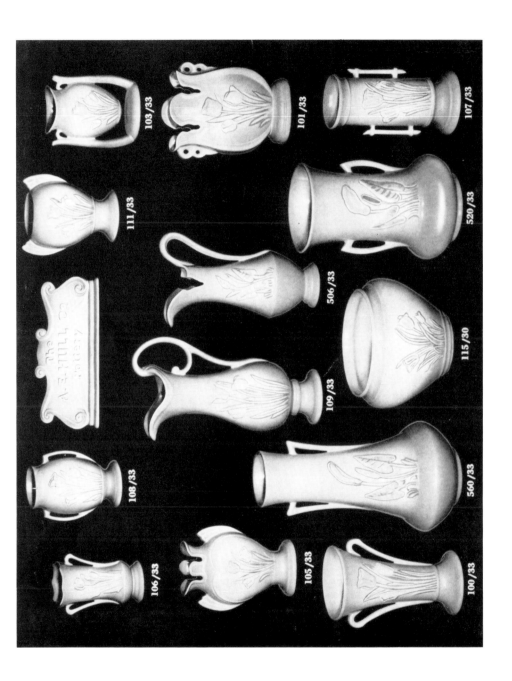

103/33

101/33

107/33

111/33

520/33

506/33

115/30

109/33

108/33

560/33

106/33

105/33

100/33

75

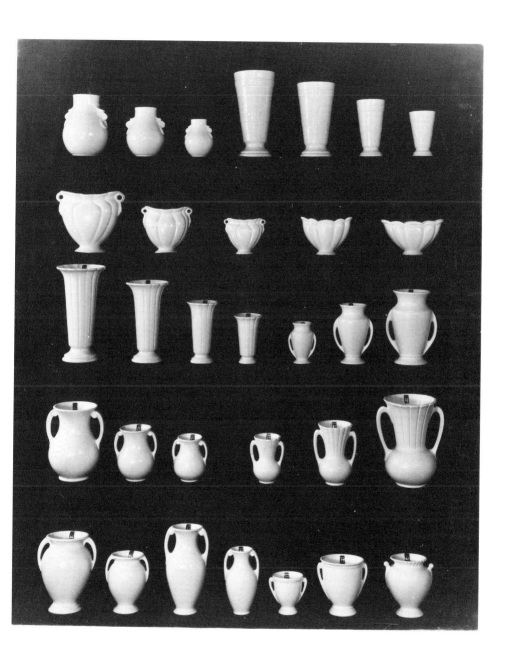

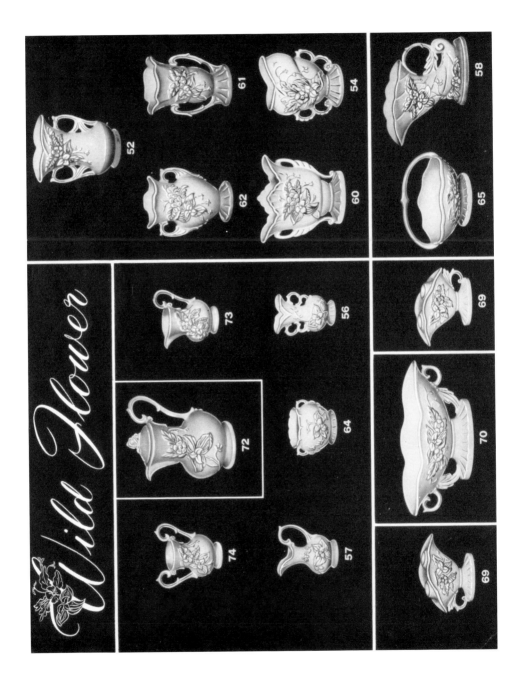

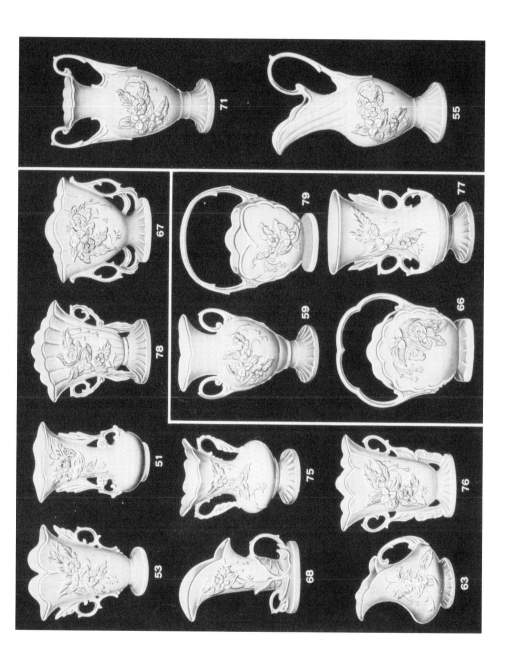

70/1.   5, 6, 7, 8, 9, 10, 11, 12, 13, 14 and 15 inch Bowls

23/2.   5, 6, 7, 8, 9, 10, 11 and 12 inch Bowls

21/2.   5, 6, 7, 8, 9, 10, 11 and 12 inch Bowls

24/2.   5, 6, 7, 8, 9, 10, 11 and 12 inch Bowls

80

5½" 6½" 7½" 8½"

9½" 10½" 11½"

SQUARE FOOT BLUE BAND SHOULDER MIXING BOWLS
No. 22/2B

RECLINING FAWN PLANTER
No. 941

4½" 5½" 6½" 7½" 8½"

9½" 10½" 11½"

BLUE BAND SHOULDER MIXING BOWLS
No. 424B

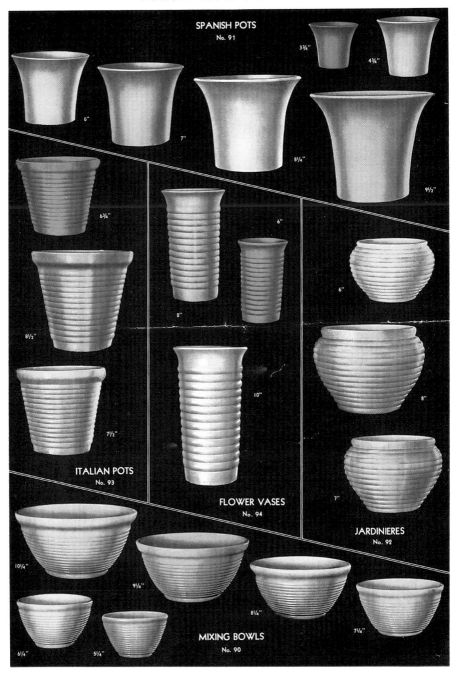

SPANISH POTS
No. 91

ITALIAN POTS
No. 93

FLOWER VASES
No. 94

JARDINIERES
No. 92

MIXING BOWLS
No. 90

No. 534.   4½ inch Jardinieres, Hand Decorated

No. 364.   4½ inch Blended Jardinieres

No. 544.   Sweet Potato or Ivy Jar with Chains

No. 539.   6½ inch Flower Pots
Saucers Attached

No. 534.   5½ inch Flower Pots with Saucers

No. 846.   7½ inch
Jardiniere

No. 546.   4, 5½, 7½ inch
Blended Jardinieres

No. 551.   7½ inch
Jardiniere

No. 550.   7½ inch
Jardiniere

No. 536.   5½ and 7½ inch Jardinieres

No. 421A.   Bowls

No. 30.   Bowls (Ovenproof)

No. 429.   Bowls (Green)

83

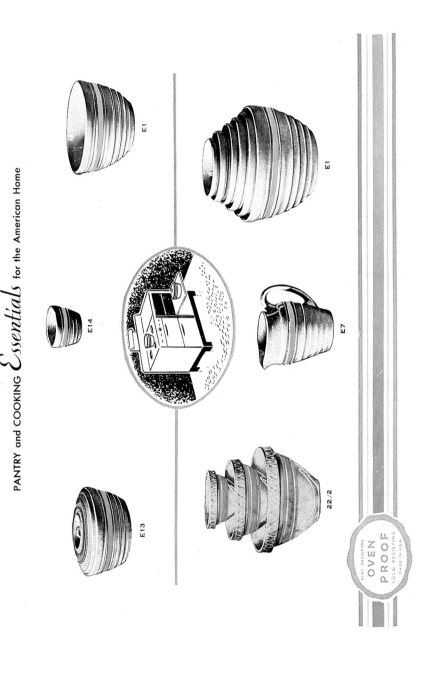

E1

E1

E14

E7

E13

22/2

OVEN PROOF
HEAT RESISTING
COLD RESISTING
MADE IN U.S.A.

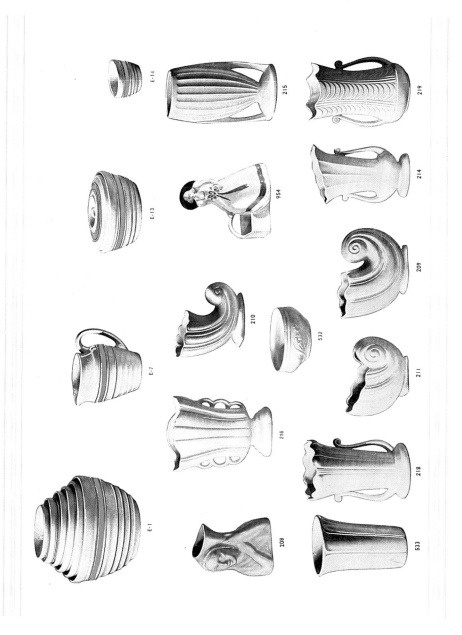

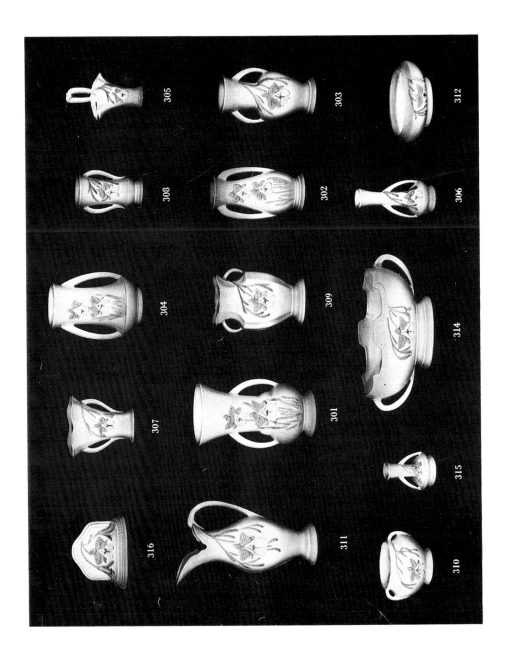

HULL POTTERY CROOKSVILLE OHIO

Florist's Ware

No. 750-9½"

No. 750-11½"

No. 750-13½"

No. 71-10"

No. 71-7"

No. 71-5"

No. 71-3¾"

No. 955
(A) ROSE
(B) BLUE

No. 954

No. 215

No. 218

No. 965

No. 219

No. 216

No. 61

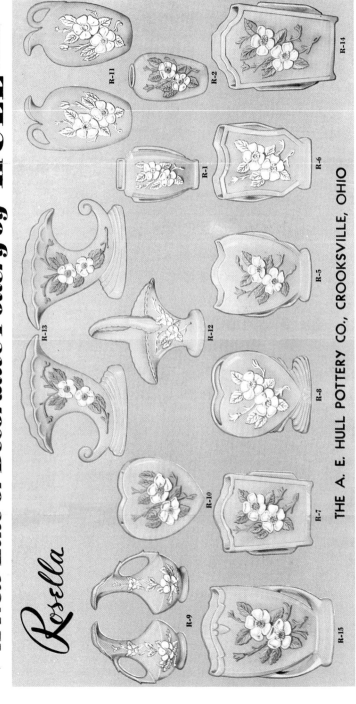

A New Line of Decorative Pottery by HULL

MASTER POTTERS

Rosella

R-11
R-2
R-14
R-1
R-6
R-13
R-5
R-12
R-10
R-8
R-7
R-9
R-15

THE A. E. HULL POTTERY CO., CROOKSVILLE, OHIO

89

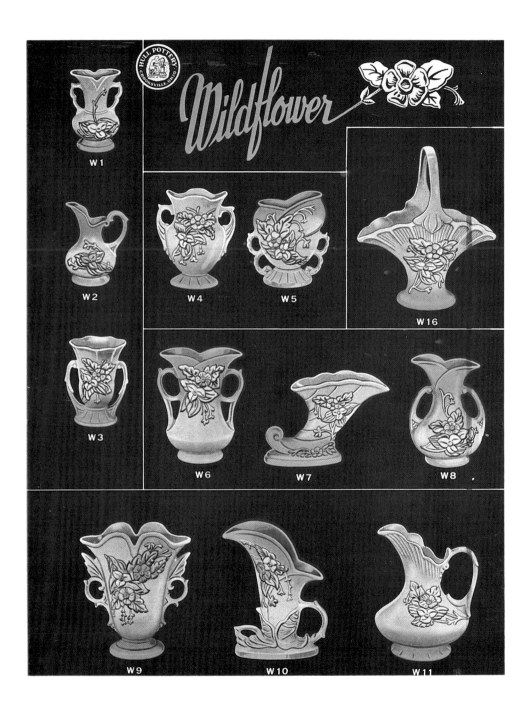

Wildflower

W 1
W 2
W 4
W 5
W 16
W 3
W 6
W 7
W 8
W 9
W 10
W 11

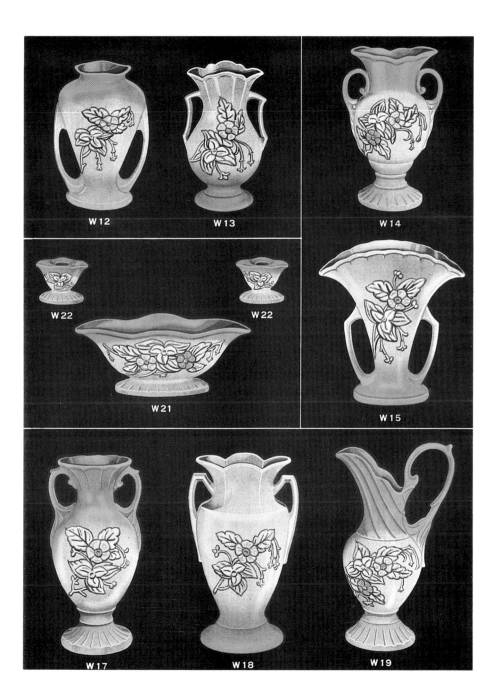

W 12   W 13   W 14

W 22   W 22

W 21

W 15

W 17   W 18   W 19

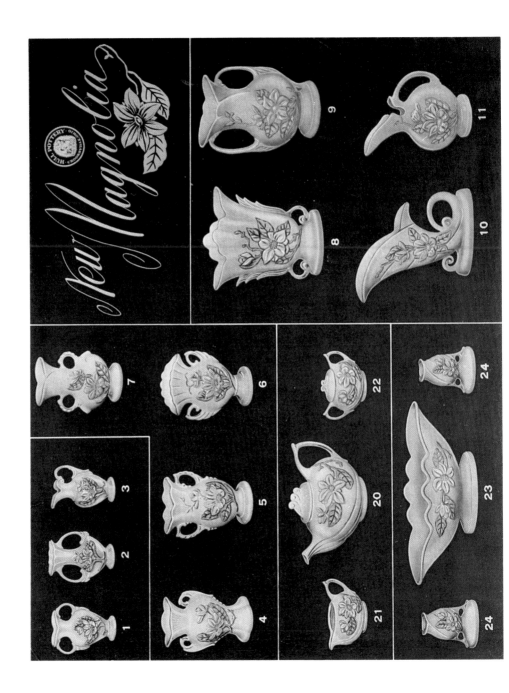

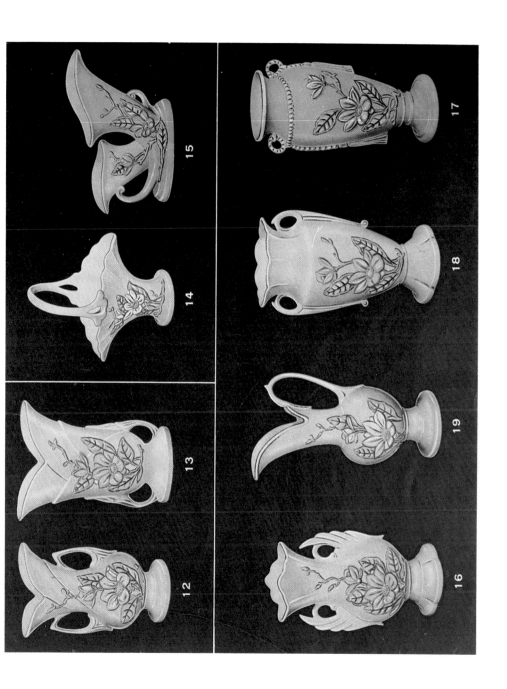

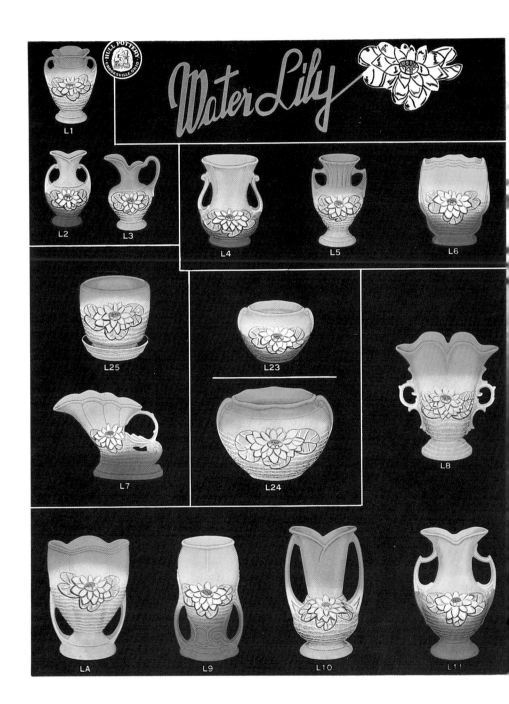

94

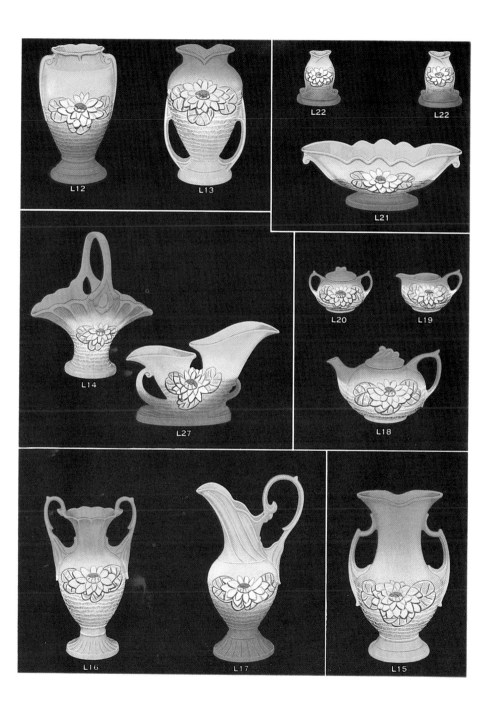

L12

L13

L22

L22

L21

L14

L27

L20

L19

L18

L16

L17

L15

HULL POTTERY
HEAT RESISTING
OVEN
PROOF
COLD RESISTING
CROOKSVILLE OHIO

Cinderella

BLOSSOM

No. 26
Tea Pot & Cover

3 Piece Tea Set

No. 27
Sugar & Cover

No. 28
Creamer

No. 29
16 oz. Pitcher

No. 24
Grease Jar & Cover

No. 22
2 qt. Ice Water Pitcher

No. 25
Pepper

No. 25
Salt

No. 29
32 oz. Pitcher

3 Piece Range Set

No. 21
7½" Baking Dish

No. 21
8½" Baking Dish

No. 21
7½" Casserole & Cover

No. 30
Cookie Jar

No. 21
8½" Casserole & Cover

No. 20
3 Piece Bowl Set
5½", 7½", & 9½"

96

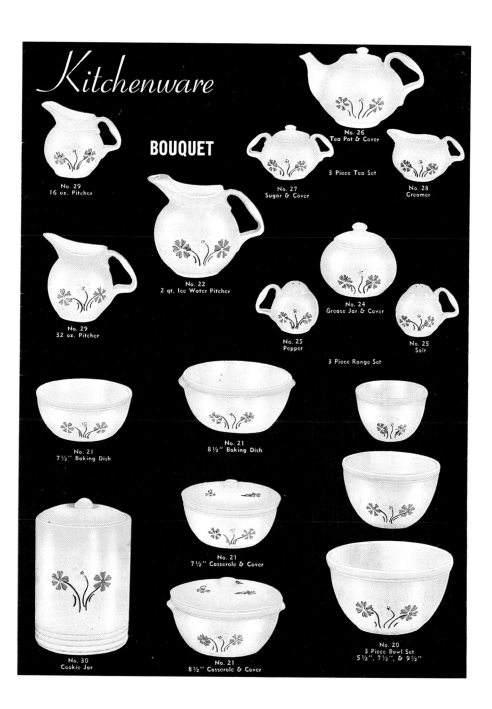

Kitchenware

BOUQUET

No. 29
16 oz. Pitcher

No. 26
Tea Pot & Cover

3 Piece Tea Set

No. 27
Sugar & Cover

No. 28
Creamer

No. 22
2 qt. Ice Water Pitcher

No. 24
Grease Jar & Cover

No. 29
32 oz. Pitcher

No. 25
Pepper

No. 25
Salt

3 Piece Range Set

No. 21
7½" Baking Dish

No. 21
8½" Baking Dish

No. 21
7½" Casserole & Cover

No. 30
Cookie Jar

No. 21
8½" Casserole & Cover

No. 20
3 Piece Bowl Set
5½", 7½", & 9½"

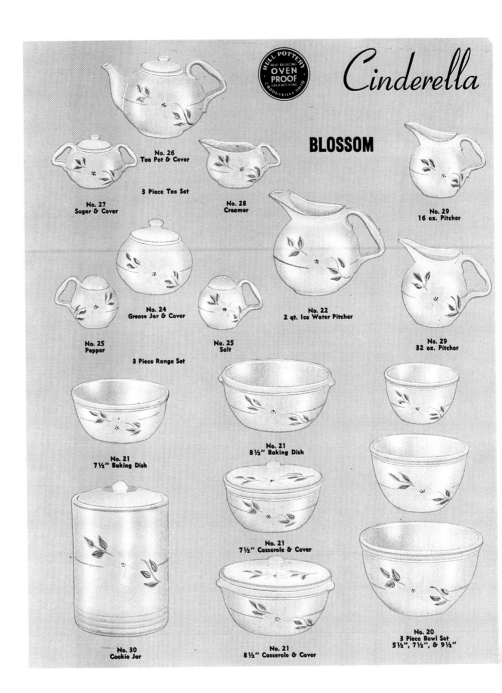

HULL POTTERY
HEAT RESISTING
OVEN PROOF
COLD RESISTING
CROOKSVILLE OHIO

Cinderella

BLOSSOM

No. 26
Tea Pot & Cover

3 Piece Tea Set

No. 27
Sugar & Cover

No. 28
Creamer

No. 29
16 oz. Pitcher

No. 24
Grease Jar & Cover

No. 22
2 qt. Ice Water Pitcher

No. 25
Pepper

No. 25
Salt

No. 29
32 oz. Pitcher

3 Piece Range Set

No. 21
7½" Baking Dish

No. 21
8½" Baking Dish

No. 21
7½" Casserole & Cover

No. 30
Cookie Jar

No. 21
8½" Casserole & Cover

No. 20
3 Piece Bowl Set
5½", 7½", & 9½"

98

Kitchenware

BOUQUET

No. 29
16 oz. Pitcher

No. 26
Tea Pot & Cover

3 Piece Tea Set

No. 27
Sugar & Cover

No. 28
Creamer

No. 22
2 qt. Ice Water Pitcher

No. 29
32 oz. Pitcher

No. 24
Grease Jar & Cover

No. 25
Pepper

No. 25
Salt

3 Piece Range Set

No. 21
7½" Baking Dish

No. 21
8½" Baking Dish

No. 21
7½" Casserole & Cover

No. 30
Cookie Jar

No. 21
8½" Casserole & Cover

No. 20
3 Piece Bowl Set
5½", 7½", & 9½"

SUN=GLOW.... *By* THE

No. 50 — 3 PIECE BOWL SET, 5½", 7½", 9½"
(Oven Proof)
Packed 6 sets, Weight 40 Pounds
Open Stock: 5½" Packed 4 Dozen, Weight 38 Pounds
7½" Packed 2 Dozen, Weight 48 Pounds
9½" Packed 1 Dozen, Weight 45 Pounds

No. 51 — 7¾" CASSEROLE WITH COVER
(Oven Proof)
Packed 1 Dozen, Weight 42 Pounds

No. 52 — 1½-PINT JUG
Packed 2 Dozen, Weight 38 Pounds

No. 53-54 — 3 PIECE RANGE SET
(Oven Proof)
Packed 12 sets, Weight 30 Pounds
Open Stock: Range Jars Packed 2 Dozen, Weight 38 Pounds
Open Stock: Salt and Peppers Packed 2 Dozen Pairs, Weight 25 Pounds

A. E. HULL POTTERY COMPANY, Inc., Crooksville, Ohio

or Decoration No. 2, Yellow

No. 80 — CUP — SAUCER WALL POCKET
Packed 2 Dozen, Weight 24 Pounds

No. 81 — JUG WALL POCKET
Packed 2 Dozen, Weight 28 Pounds

No. 82 — WHISK BROOM WALL POCKET
Packed 2 Dozen, Weight 30 Pounds

No. 83 IRON PLANTER — WALL POCKET
Packed 1 Dozen, Weight 16 Pounds

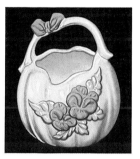

No. 84 — BASKET
Packed 1 Dozen, Weight 20 Pounds

No. 85 — 8½" VASE
Packed 1 Dozen, Weight 30 Pounds

No. 86 — TEA BELL
Packed 2 Dozen, Weight 15 Pounds

No. 87 — TEA BELL
Packed 2 Dozen, Weight 20 Pounds

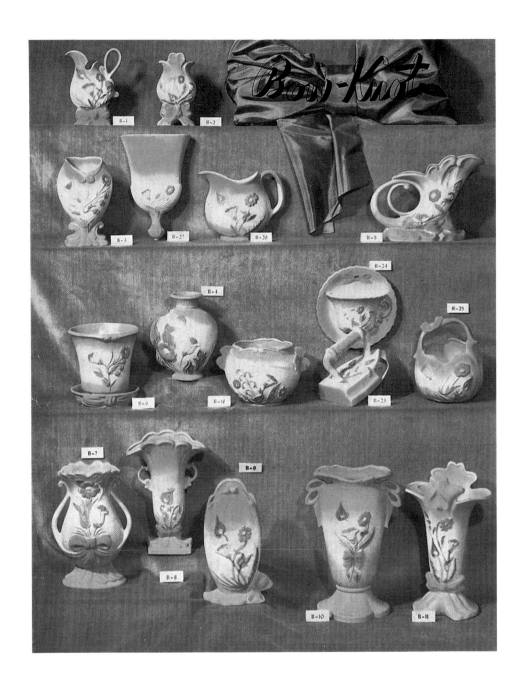

by
THE A. E. HULL
POTTERY CO.
Crooksville, Ohio

B-20

B-23

B-21

B-12

B-13

B-16

B-29

B-17

B-28

B-19

B-14

B-15

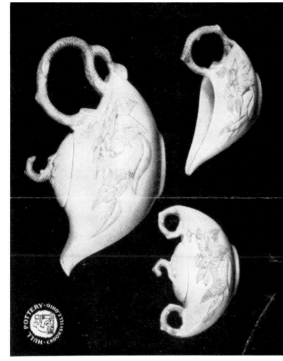
104

Woodland

The A. E. Hull Pottery Co., Inc.
CROOKSVILLE, OHIO

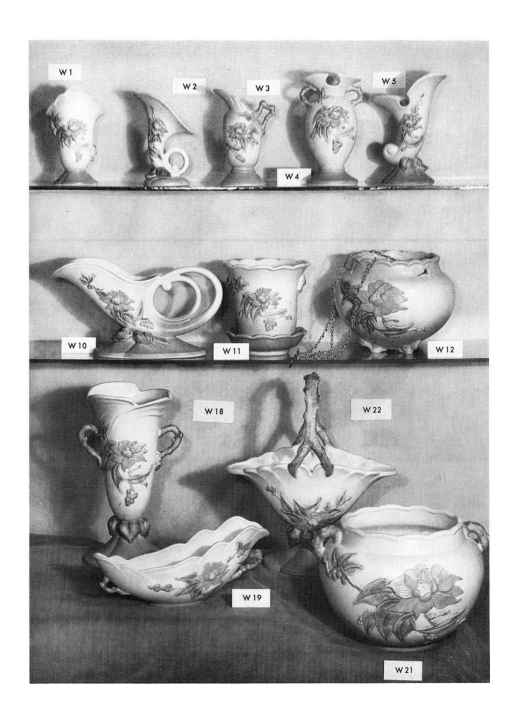

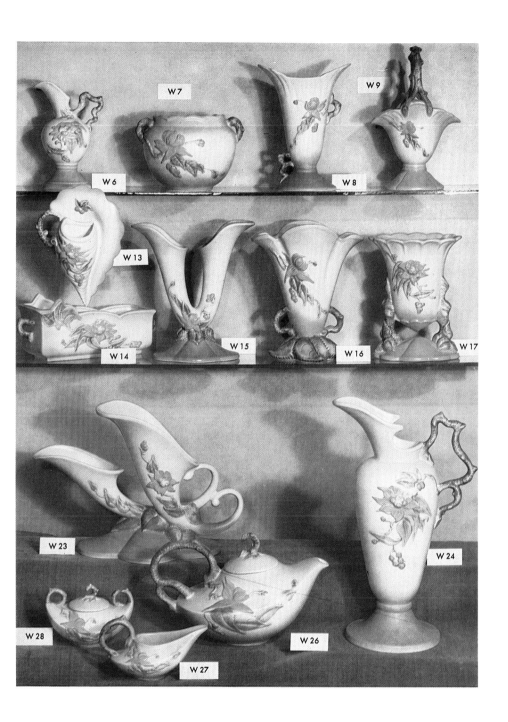

The NEW
HI-GLOSS *Woodland*

Hull Pottery Co. CROOKSVILLE, OHIO

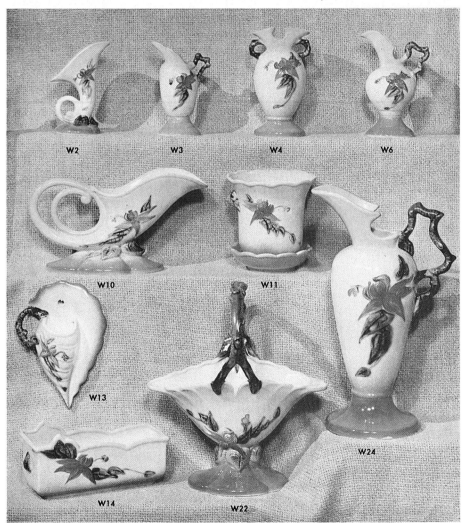

W2 W3 W4 W6

W10 W11

W13

W14 W22

W24

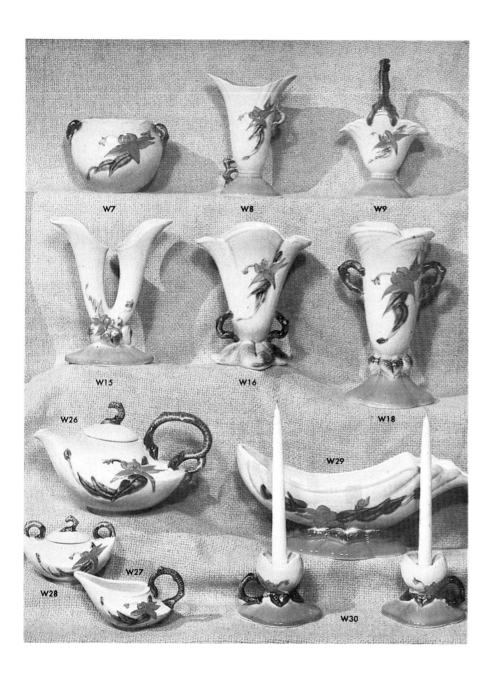

W7 W8 W9

W15 W16 W18

W26 W29

W27

W28 W30

109

Woodland

Hull Pottery Co. CROOKSVILLE, OHIO

W7 W8 W9

W15 W16

W18

W26

W29

W27

W28

W30

111

NEW
"Parchment and Pine"
by HULL

Scrolls of Parchment — for centuries, mankind's only method of passing its knowledge on to future generations — now serves as the basic design motif in Hull's new "Parchment and Pine" patterns.

Parchment . . . repeatedly varnished to preserve priceless contents, rolled, and yellowed with age . . . lends its gracefully curved beauty to this fine art pottery, with just the right touch of texture and color provided by clusters of pine and cones.

You'll like "Parchment and Pine" — by Hull.

Hull Pottery Co.

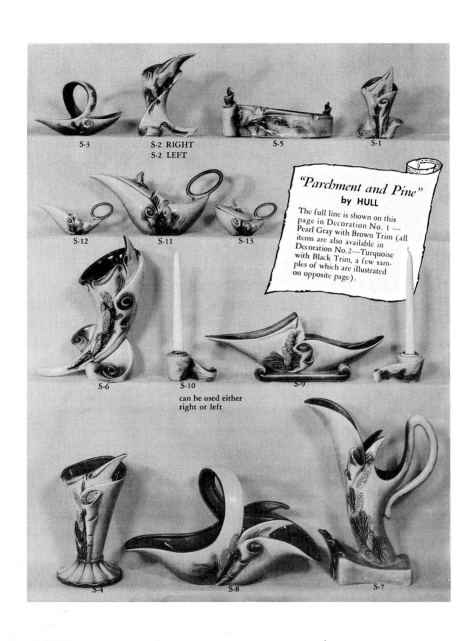

S-3

S-2 RIGHT
S-2 LEFT

S-5

S-1

S-12

S-11

S-13

"Parchment and Pine"
by HULL

The full line is shown on this page in Decoration No. 1 — Pearl Gray with Brown Trim (all items are also available in Decoration No. 2 — Turquoise with Black Trim, a few samples of which are illustrated on opposite page).

S-6

S-10

can be used either
right or left

S-9

S-4

S-8

S-7

Crooksville, Ohio

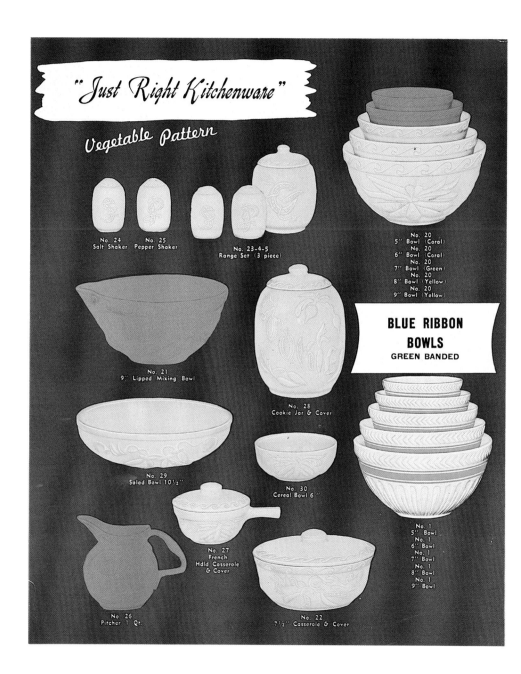

"Just Right Kitchenware"

Vegetable Pattern

No. 24
Salt Shaker

No. 25
Pepper Shaker

No. 23-4-5
Range Set (3 piece)

No. 20
5" Bowl (Coral)
No. 20
6" Bowl (Coral)
No. 20
7" Bowl (Green)
No. 20
8" Bowl (Yellow)
No. 20
9" Bowl (Yellow)

No. 21
9" Lipped Mixing Bowl

No. 28
Cookie Jar & Cover

BLUE RIBBON
BOWLS
GREEN BANDED

No. 29
Salad Bowl 10½"

No. 30
Cereal Bowl 6"

No. 27
French
Hdld Casserole
& Cover

No. 26
Pitcher 1 Qt.

No. 22
7½" Casserole & Cover

No. 1
5" Bowl
No. 1
6" Bowl
No. 1
7" Bowl
No. 1
8" Bowl
No. 1
9" Bowl

"*Just Right Kitchenware*"

Floral Pattern

No. 44
Salt Shaker

No. 45
Pepper Shaker

No. 43-4-5
Range Set (3 piece)

No. 40
5" Mixing Bowls

No. 40
6" Mixing Bowls

No. 40
7" Mixing Bowls

No. 40
8" Mixing Bowls

No. 40
9" Mixing Bowls

No. 47
French Hdld Casserole
Open

No. 48
Cookie Jar & Cover

No. 47
French Hdld Casserole
& Cover

No. 42
7½" Casserole & Cover

No. 50
Cereal Bowl 6"

No. 41
9" Lipped Mixing
Bowl also available
but not illustrated.

No. 49
Salad Bowl 10½"

No. 46
Pitcher 1 Qt.

HULL POTTERY Co. - Crooksville, Ohio

$\mathcal{D}ebonair$ · Oven-Proof Kitchenware

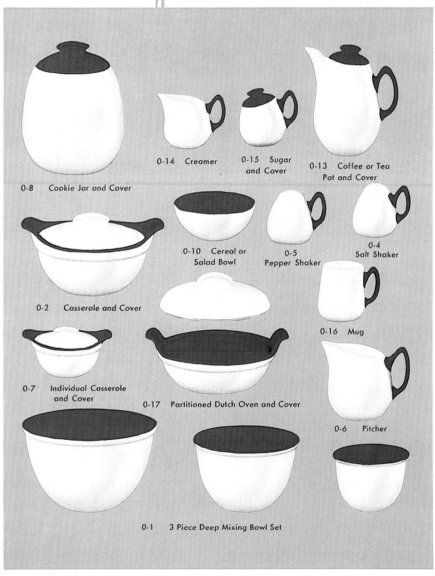

0-8 Cookie Jar and Cover

0-14 Creamer

0-15 Sugar and Cover

0-13 Coffee or Tea Pot and Cover

0-2 Casserole and Cover

0-10 Cereal or Salad Bowl

0-5 Pepper Shaker

0-4 Salt Shaker

0-16 Mug

0-7 Individual Casserole and Cover

0-17 Partitioned Dutch Oven and Cover

0-6 Pitcher

0-1 3 Piece Deep Mixing Bowl Set

Hull Pottery Co. CROOKSVILLE, OHIO

Crescent OVEN-PROOF KITCHENWARE

B16 - Mug (12 oz.)

B13J - Ice Jug

B8 - Cookie Jar and Cover

B15 - Creamer

B14 - Sugar and Cover

B2 - Casserole and Cover (10″ over-all)

B7 - Individual Casserole and Cover (6¼″ over-all)

B5 - Pepper Shaker

B4 - Salt Shaker

B13 - Teapot and Cover (6 cup)

B1 - 9½″ Mixing Bowl

B1 - 7½″ Mixing Bowl

B1 - 5½″ Mixing Bowl or Cereal Bowl

Hull Pottery Co. CROOKSVILLE, OHIO

E-9
11 ¾" Cornucopia

E-10
14" Pitcher

E-11
16½" x 8¾" Basket

E-12
15¾" x 9" Console Bowl

E-6
9¼" Angel Fish

E-5
6⅛" x 9⅛" Basket

E-13
Candle Holder

E-8
Ash Tray

E-7
11" Fish Vase

E-2
7" Twin Fish Vase

E-14
Tea Pot & Cover

E-16
Sugar & Cover

E-4
8¼" Pitcher Vase

E-15
Creamer

E-1
7" Bud Vase

E-3
7½" Cornucopia

HULL

E-12
15¾" x 9" Console Bowl

E-13
Candle Holder

E-6
9¼" Angel Fish

E-2
11¾" Cornucopia

E-14
Tea Pot & Cover

E-15
Creamer

E-3
7½" Cornucopia

E-16
Sugar & Cover

Ebb Tide ... by Hull

Up from the sea comes the inspiration for Hull's newest, colorful, complete line of art pottery. In Ebb Tide, the shapes that inhabit the seas . . . shells, coral, fish, and plants . . . set the motif. Hull has captured them, in glowing colors, and fashioned them into art pottery of great beauty.

EBB TIDE is available in two decorations. The complete 16 piece line is illustrated, left, in Decoration 2 — Wine & Seaweed. The entire 16 piece line is also available in Decoration 1 — Shrimp & Turquoise, in which some representative samples are illustrated immediately above.

BLOSSOM FLITE... by HULL

As a summer storm subsides, the land is flooded with the rosy light of the reappearing sun, and a final gust of wind detaches flower petals from their stems to fill the air with form and color.

This magic, fleeting moment in nature has been captured permanently by Hull to set the theme for BLOSSOM FLITE. As the design motif for this entire line of enchanting art pottery, BLOSSOM FLITE presents a distinctive new rendering, yet stays within the bounds of the vastly popular floral theme.

The full line of BLOSSOM FLITE is available in two basic color schemes. Decoration A is the currently popular Charcoal Gray and Pink, a few representative pieces of which are illustrated on this page. The full line, illustrated on opposite page, is shown in Decoration B, a pace-setting combination of Blue and Metallic Green.

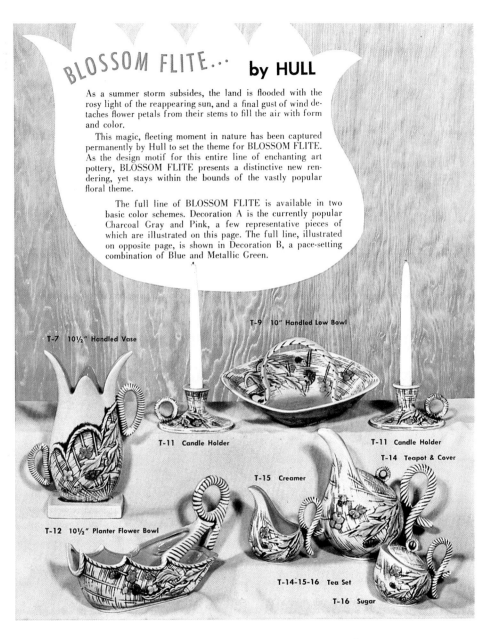

T-9   10" Handled Low Bowl

T-7   10½" Handled Vase

T-11   Candle Holder

T-11   Candle Holder

T-14   Teapot & Cover

T-15   Creamer

T-12   10½" Planter Flower Bowl

T-14-15-16   Tea Set

T-16   Sugar

Hull Pottery Company - -

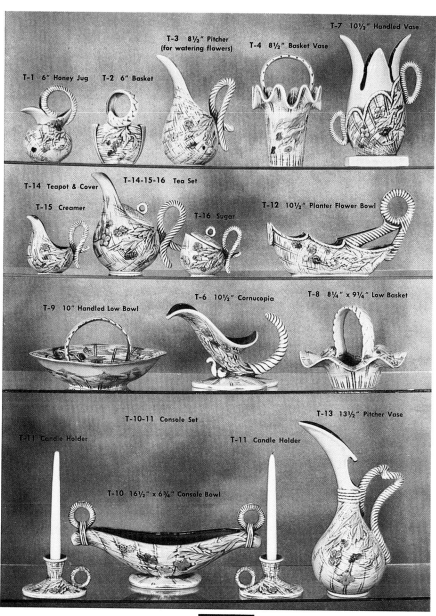

T-1 6" Honey Jug   T-2 6" Basket

T-3 8½" Pitcher
(for watering flowers)

T-4 8½" Basket Vase

T-7 10½" Handled Vase

T-14 Teapot & Cover

T-14-15-16 Tea Set

T-15 Creamer

T-16 Sugar

T-12 10½" Planter Flower Bowl

T-9 10" Handled Low Bowl

T-6 10½" Cornucopia

T-8 8¼" x 9¼" Low Basket

T-10-11 Console Set

T-13 13½" Pitcher Vase

T-11 Candle Holder

T-11 Candle Holder

T-10 16½" x 6¾" Console Bowl

Crooksville, Ohio

121

B1—6¼"
Bud Vase

B2—6¼"
Cornucopia

B3—7"
Ash Tray

B4—6½"
Bon Bon Dish

B5—5" x 6"
Jardiniere

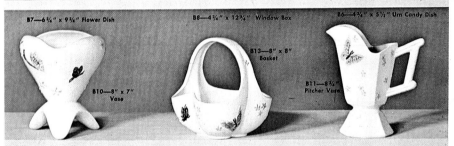

B7—6¾" x 9¾" Flower Dish

B8—4¾" x 12¾" Window Box

B6—4¾" x 5½" Urn Candy Dish

B13—8" x 8"
Basket

B10—8" x 7"
Vase

B11—8¾"
Pitcher Vase

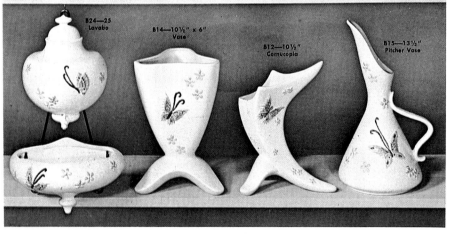

B24—25
Lavabo

B14—10½" x 6"
Vase

B12—10½"
Cornucopia

B15—13½"
Pitcher Vase

Hull P

NEW *Butterfly* ART POTTERY *by* Hull

Colorful butterflies flutter through pastel flowers in this newest entrancing collection by Hull. The varied shapes range from classic to modern, yet the BUTTERFLY design motif integrates them all into a wide line of matched art pottery . . . America's finest, from the kilns of Hull.

Two decorations are available in BUTTERFLY. Decoration No. 1 is a startlingly beautiful White-on-White (Opaque Gloss White spattered on a Mat Transparent White, with Butterflies and Flowers in pastels under the glaze) illustrated opposite. Decoration No. 2, Turquoise, shown on this page, features colored inner surfaces and a smooth transparent mat glaze over all. All pieces illustrated here are available in either decoration.

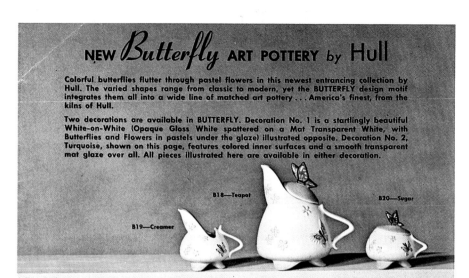

B18—Teapot

B19—Creamer

B20—Sugar

B23—11½" Serving Tray

B9—9" Vase

B16—4¾" x 10½" Fruit Bowl

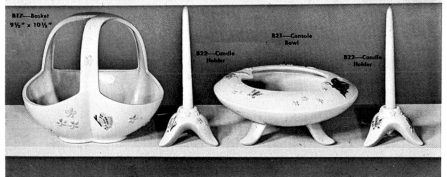

B17—Basket
9½" x 10½"

B22—Candle
Holder

B21—Console
Bowl

B22—Candle
Holder

ottery Company - - Crooksville, Ohio

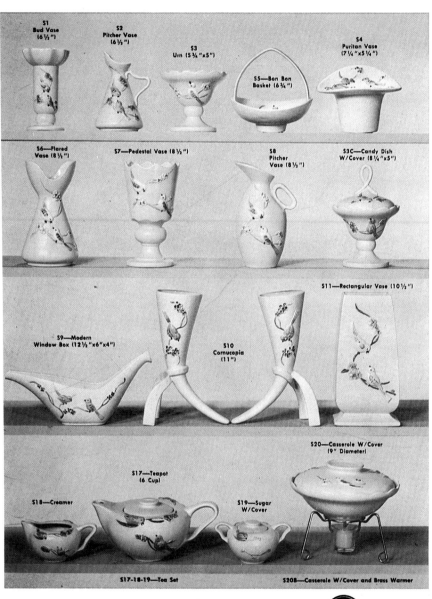

S1
Bud Vase
(6½")

S2
Pitcher Vase
(6½")

S3
Urn (5¾"x5")

S5—Bon Bon
Basket (6¾")

S4
Puritan Vase
(7¼"x5¼")

S6—Flared
Vase (8½")

S7—Pedestal Vase (8½")

S8
Pitcher
Vase (8½")

S3C—Candy Dish
W/Cover (8¼"x5")

S9—Modern
Window Box (12½"x6"x4")

S10
Cornucopia
(11")

S11—Rectangular Vase (10½")

S20—Casserole W/Cover
(9" Diameter)

S17—Teapot
(6 Cup)

S18—Creamer

S19—Sugar
W/Cover

S17-18-19—Tea Set

S20B—Casserole W/Cover and Brass Warmer

Printed in U. S. A.

ght 1957 by Hull Pottery Co.

 *Hull P*

124

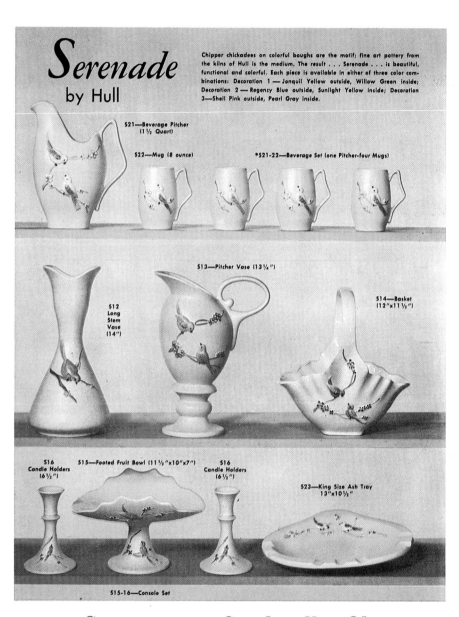

Serenade by Hull

Chipper chickadees on colorful boughs are the motif; fine art pottery from the kilns of Hull is the medium. The result . . . Serenade . . . is beautiful, functional and colorful. Each piece is available in either of three color combinations: Decoration 1 — Jonquil Yellow outside, Willow Green inside; Decoration 2 — Regency Blue outside, Sunlight Yellow inside; Decoration 3—Shell Pink outside, Pearl Gray inside.

S21—Beverage Pitcher (1 ½ Quart)

S22—Mug (8 ounce)

*S21-22—Beverage Set (one Pitcher-four Mugs)

S13—Pitcher Vase (13¼")

S12 Long Stem Vase (14")

S14—Basket (12"x11½")

S16 Candle Holders (6½")

S15—Footed Fruit Bowl (11½"x10"x7")

S16 Candle Holders (6½")

S23—King Size Ash Tray 13"x10½"

S15-16—Console Set

ottery Company - - Crooksville, Ohio

Hull Heritageware...

The accent is on Kitchenware...by Hull

Featuring the modern "light touch of foam!"

▶ Available in Mint Green and Azure Blue for new color-coordinated magic.

▶ Oven-proof, refrigerator-proof...useful accessories for every kitchen.

▶ New "Americana Modern"...the traditional approach to modern design...fits any kitchen decor.

Five-piece SALAD SET. One 10" salad bowl and four "personal size" 5¾" bowls. Ideal for soups, cereals or desserts. Set, A-9. Packed 4 complete sets per carton.

Three-piece WAFFLE SET includes 7½" bowl, 28-ounce pitcher and small 8-ounce pitcher with "no-drip" lips. Pitchers can be used for serving milk, ice water or fruit juices. 7½" bowl, A-1. 28-oz. pitcher, A-7. 8-oz. pitcher, A-7. Packed 4 sets per carton.

Three-piece RANGE SET... consists of range jar and matched salt and pepper shakers. Set can be used at range or at the table. Range jar and cover A-3. Salt shaker, A-4. Pepper shaker, A-5. Packed 4 sets per carton.

9 oz. MUGS with large-size handles. The modern way to serve soups. Keeps cold drinks colder, hot drinks better... longer. Packed 12 per carton. A-8.

CRUET SET... consists of oil and vinegar bottles with stoppers. Use for all dressings. Oil bottle, A-14. Vinegar bottle, A-15. Packed 6 sets per carton.

Three-piece BOWL SET. 6½", 7½" and 8½" bowls. Ideal for mixing or for vegetable serving dishes. Stacks easily, saves cupboard space. Set, A-1. Packed 4 sets per carton.

Family-size COOKIE JAR with cover. Wide mouth opening, stores "loads of cookies," easy to clean. Packed 4 per carton. A-18.

Oven-proof CASSEROLE and server. Moves gracefully from oven to table. Convertible cover becomes its own trivet, serving as base for casserole. Can be used as attractive center-piece. Modern scalloped edged design. Packed 4 per carton. A-2.

Hull designers styled these pieces for versatility. Heritageware has 101 uses around the home ... each piece can be used in many different ways for attractive table settings, to make home meal planning easier and more convenient. Ready for immediate shipment. Assorted colors at no extra cost.

Display Heritageware in planned groups and it will sell on sight. Rapid turnover brings extra profits ... with colorful, attractive Hull pottery. See the entire line of profit-building Hull pottery for the home. Hull ... famous for pottery since 1905.

Hull Pottery Company • Crooksville, Ohio

Printed in U.S.A.
Copyright 1958, Hull Pottery Co.

126

No. 10
Cornucopia 11"
(Reversible)

No. 13
Pitcher Vase 12"

No. 11
Moon Basket 10½"

No. 2
Two Handled Vase
6"

No. 3
Pitcher Vase 8"

No. 1
Cornucopia 6½"
(Reversible)

No. 15
Basket 12"

No. 12
Two Hdld. Spool Vase
12"

No. 6
Basket 8"

Hull

128

TOKAY . . . with striking colors under mirror-glaze FINISH
. . . covers every art pottery requirement, yet
consists of only 18 basic pieces. It's easy to
stock, to sell profitably and frequently.
Another Masterpiece Line from The Kilns of Hull.

No. 17
Creamer

No. 16
Teapot (6 Cup)

No. 18
Sugar W/Cover

No. 9
Planter 5½"x6½"

No. 16-17-18
Tea Set

No. 9C
Candy Dish W/Cover
7"x8½"

No. 14
Consolette 15¾"

No. 5
Urn 5½"x5½"

No. 8
Two Handled Vase
10"

No. 4
Two Handled Vase
8¼"

No. 7
Fruit Bowl 9½"

Pottery Company - - Crooksville, Ohio

"TUSCANY" pattern by **HULL**

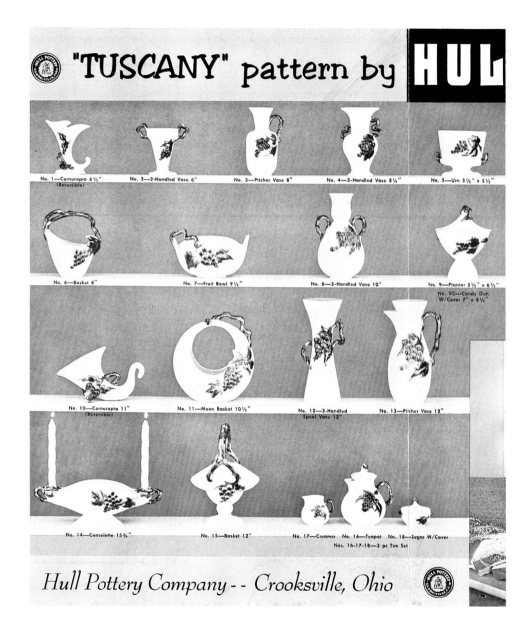

No. 1—Cornucopia 6½" (Reversible) No. 2—2-Handled Vase 6" No. 3—Pitcher Vase 8" No. 4—2-Handled Vase 8¼" No. 5—Urn 5½" x 5½"

No. 6—Basket 8" No. 7—Fruit Bowl 9½" No. 8—2-Handled Vase 10" No. 9—Planter 5½" x 6½" No. 9C—Candy Dish W/Cover 7" x 8½"

No. 10—Cornucopia 11" (Reversible) No. 11—Moon Basket 10½" No. 12—2-Handled Spool Vase 12" No. 13—Pitcher Vase 12"

No. 14—Consolette 15¾" No. 15—Basket 12" No. 17—Creamer No. 16—Teapot No. 18—Sugar W/Cover Nos. 16-17-18—3 pc Tea Set

Hull Pottery Company - - Crooksville, Ohio

130

TUSCANY, known as the Garden of Italy,

is the inspiration for this beautiful expression

of the potters art. Ornamented in relief

with grapes and leaves from the valley of the

silver Arno, bringing the peasant art

of Italy to the homes of America.

DECORATION 1—*Sweet Pink with embossed grapes and leaves in fashionable Gray-Green.*

DECORATION 2—*Milk White with embossed grapes and leaves in cool Forest Green.*

NEW! additions to "TUSCANY" pattern by HULL

No. 21 15" Handled Slender-Neck Vase

No. 20 15" Footed Decorator Vase

No. 19 14" x 10½" Leaf Flower Bowl

All three shapes available in Pink or Milk White with embossed motif in fashionable green.

Hull Pottery Company
CROOKSVILLE, OHIO

Tropicana

Hand Decorated pieces - -
carefree and colorful like
the happy days of a Caribbean
Holiday. Beautiful and unusual
shapes in pottery - - hand painted
with gay figures against a white
background edged in Tropic Green.

No. T57
14½" Planter Vase

No. T56
12½" Pitcher Vase

No. T55
12¾" Fancy Basket

No. T54
12½" Slender Vase

No. T53
8½" Flat-Sided
Vase

No. T51
15½" x 4¾"
Flower Bowl

No. T52
10" x 7½"
Ash Tray

Hull Pottery Company - - Crooksville, Ohio

Continental

PERSIMMON--

the completely captivating accent for today's interiors in the higher key of contemporary color.

No. C60—15" Pedestal Vase
No. C59—15" Slender Neck Vase
No. C63—14" x 10½" Caladium Leaf
No. C62C—8½" Candy Dish with Cover
No. C51—15½" x 4¾" Flower Dish
No. C61—10" Two Purpose Vase
No. C52—10" x 7½" Ash Tray
No. C56—12½" Pitcher Vase

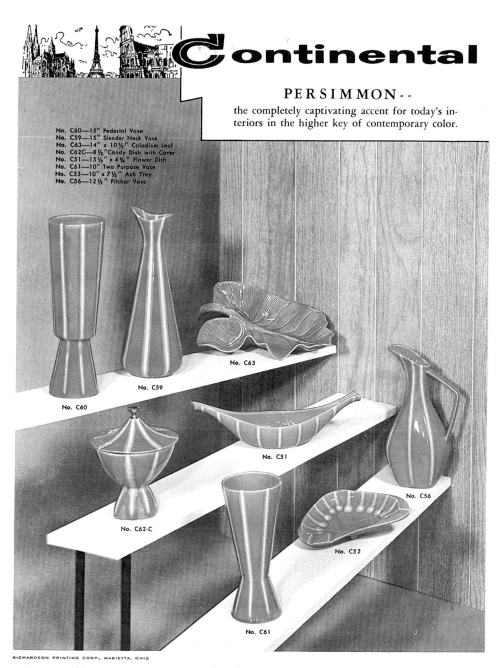

No. C60

No. C59

No. C63

No. C62-C

No. C51

No. C56

No. C52

No. C61

RICHARDSON PRINTING CORP., MARIETTA, OHIO

Hull Pottery Company -- Crooksville, Ohio

Lovely natural colors - - -
accented with rich, bold stripes

EVERGREEN - -
a delightfully subtle color that lends itself as a perfect
foil to nature's own brilliant floral and leaf displays.

No. C55—12¾" Basket
No. C58—13¾" Vase

No. C55

No. C58

No. C61—10" Two Purpose Vase
(Shown as Candleholder)
No. C54—12½" Free Form Vase
No. C53—8½" Vase
No. C62—5½" x 6¾" Footed Compote or
Planter

No. C61

No. C54

No. C53

No. C62

No. C57

No. A20

No. A1

No. C57—14½" Open
Front Vase
No. A20—10" Free Form
Ash Tray w/Pen
No. A1—8" Ash Tray

Continental - - - beauty that comes from expert
craftsmanship, modern designs and finest glazes.

New **Continental**

Sophisticated, Modern Shapes In Three Delightful Decorator Colors.

MOUNTAIN BLUE Imagine twilight in the Blue Mountains— modernized with stripes of white haze.

No. C64   No. C66   No. C70   No. C28   No. C29

No. C69   No. C67   No. C68   No. C67

No. A3   No. A40

No. C64—10″ Open Front Vase
No. C66—9½″ Bud Vase
No. C70—13¼″ Consolette
No. C28—9¾″ Rose Vase

No. C29—12″ Rose Vase
No. C69—9¼″ Open Footed Flower Bowl
No. C67—4″ Sq. Ftd. Planter/Candle Holder
No. C68—8½″ x 4½″ Rectangular Ftd. Planter

No. C67-68—3 Piece Console Set
No. A3—12″ Pinched Rectangular Ash Tray
No. A40—13″ Oval Ash Tray W/Pen

Hull Pottery Company - - Crooksville, Ohio

An Exciting New

No. C525—Pitcher Vase 6¼" High
No. C49—Lion Head Urn Vase 5¾"
No. C50—Lion Head Urn Vase 9"
No. C29—Rose Vase 12"
No. C87—Pine Cone Pitcher Vase 12"
No. C80—Llama Planter
No. C47C—Bon Bon Bowl w/Cover
No. C314—Flying Duck Planter
No. C46—Scalloped Fl. Bowl 4½"x8"
No. C14—Pillow Vase 6"x3¼"x4"

No. C62—Compote 5½"x6¾"
No. C15—Oval Ped. Vase 5¾"x5½"
No. C67—Square Footed Planter 4"
No. C68—Rect. Flower Dish 8½"x4½"
No. C67-68—Three Piece Console Set
No. C44—Round Fl. Bowl 4¼"x5¾"

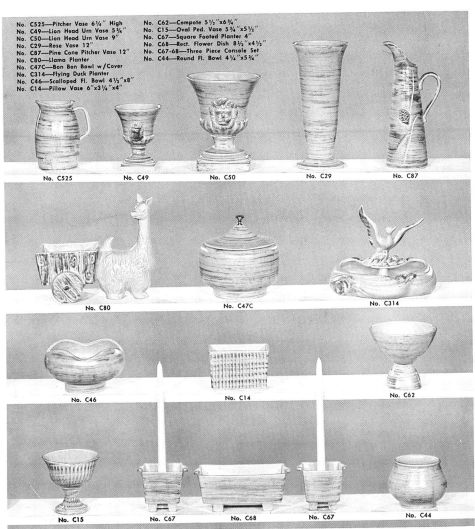

No. C525   No. C49   No. C50   No. C29   No. C87

No. C80   No. C47C   No. C314

No. C46   No. C14   No. C62

No. C15   No. C67   No. C68   No. C67   No. C44

Hull Pottery Company, Crooksville, Ohio

Hand Decorated Line of Art Pottery Inspired by the Isle of the Sun

<u>CORAL</u> *The antique beauty of weathered limestone—a lovely cameo finish captured in pottery designed for the discerning buyer.*

| No. C28 | No. C59 | No. C58 | No. C57 | No. C64 |

| No. C81 | No. C45 | No. C62C | No. C38 | No. C47 |

| No. C52 | No. C48 | No. C63 |

| No. C21 | No. C23 | No. C21 |

No. C28—Rose Vase 9¾"
No. C59—Slender Neck Vase 15"
No. C58—Vase 13¾"
No. C57—Open Front Vase 14½"
No. C64—Open Front Vase 10"
No. C81—Twin Swan Planter

No. C45—Ribbed Flower Bowl 4¼"x6"
No. C62C—Candy Dish w/Cover 8½"
No. C38—Basket 6¾"x6"
No. C47—Fld. Rd. Flower Bowl 5¼"x8"
No. C52—Ash Tray 10"x7½"

No. C48—Leaf Basket 12¼"x5½"
No. C63—Caladium Leaf 14"x10½"
No. C21—Baby Swan Planter 4"x3"
No. C23—Lg. Swan Planter 8½"x7"x6"
No. C21-23—Three Piece Swan Plt. Set

Hull Pottery Co. CROOKSVILLE, OHIO

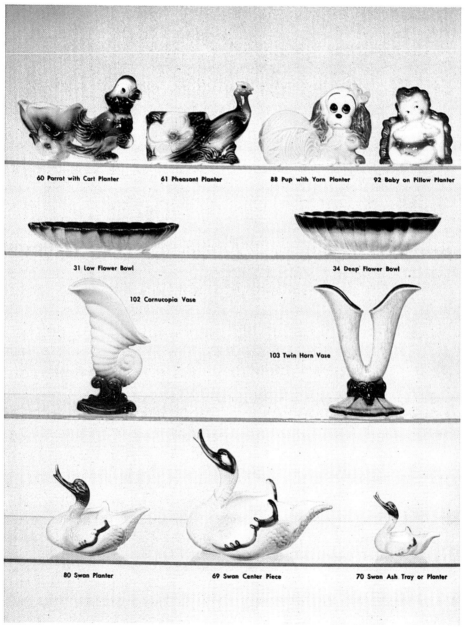

60 Parrot with Cart Planter   61 Pheasant Planter   88 Pup with Yarn Planter   92 Baby on Pillow Planter

31 Low Flower Bowl   34 Deep Flower Bowl

102 Cornucopia Vase

103 Twin Horn Vase

80 Swan Planter   69 Swan Center Piece   70 Swan Ash Tray or Planter

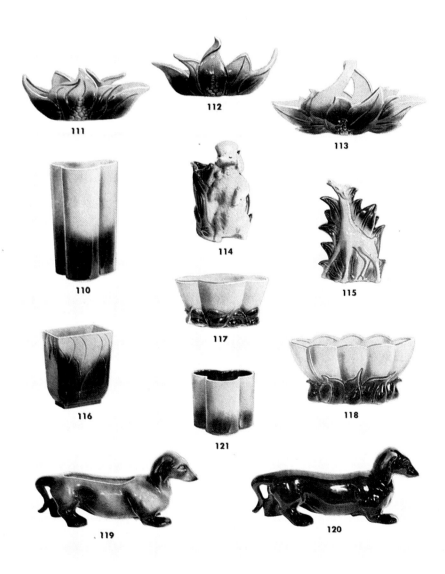

Hull Pottery Co. CROOKSVILLE, OHIO

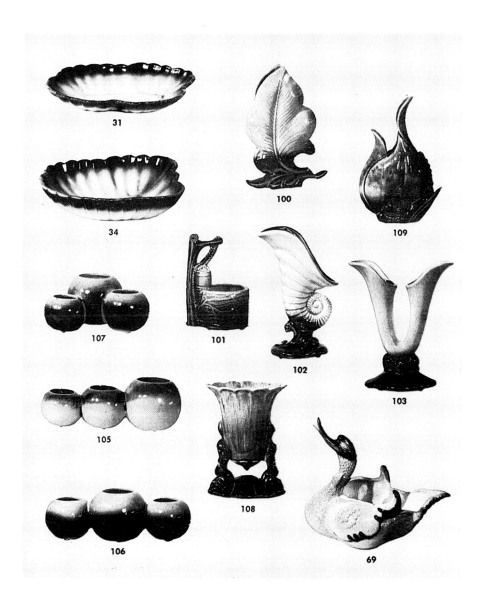

141

Hull Pottery Co. CROOKSVILLE, OHIO

53 Rooster Planter
(5¼")

54 Rooster Center Piece or Planter
(9")

55 Knight on Horseback Planter

57 Twin Deer Vase
(8¼")

62 Twin Deer Vase
(11¼")

59 Colt on Flower Bowl

64 Cornucopia Planter

67 Flying Goose Wall Pocket or Planter

125 Colt Figurine

71 Scroll Window Bowl

73 Scalloped Garden Dish
(14¾")

82 Scalloped Garden Dish
(12¾")

78 Leaf Shaped Flower Bowl

126 Modern Flower Bowl

79 Flying Duck
Planter

63 Siamese Cat with Kitten Planter

66 Lamb Planter

56 Scroll Basket
(9")

72 Scroll Basket
(12½")

Hull Pottery Co. CROOKSVILLE, OHIO

110 Clover Shaped Vase

111 Novelty Window Box

113 Handled Planter Basket

114 French Poodle Vase

115 Giraffe Vase

116 Rectangular Vase

117 Oval Flower Bowl

118 Deep Oval Flower Bowl

121 Clover Shaped Planter

122 Handled Basket

124 Rectangular Flower Dish

81 Double Hippo Planter

Hull Pottery Co. CROOKSVILLE, OHIO

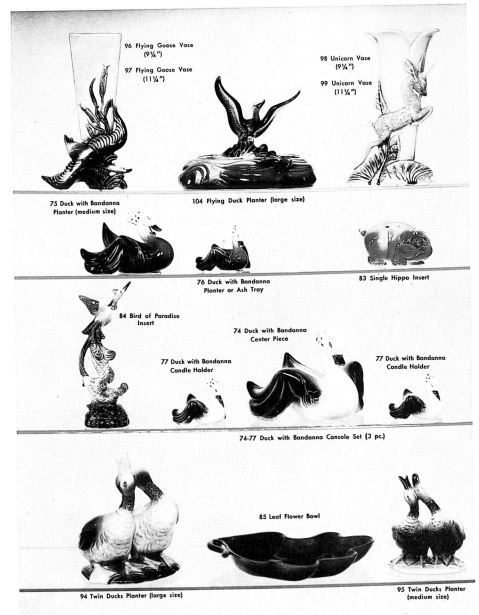

96 Flying Goose Vase
(9¼")

97 Flying Goose Vase
(11¼")

98 Unicorn Vase
(9¼")

99 Unicorn Vase
(11¼")

75 Duck with Bandanna
Planter (medium size)

104 Flying Duck Planter (large size)

76 Duck with Bandanna
Planter or Ash Tray

83 Single Hippo Insert

84 Bird of Paradise
Insert

74 Duck with Bandanna
Center Piece

77 Duck with Bandanna
Candle Holder

77 Duck with Bandanna
Candle Holder

74-77 Duck with Bandanna Console Set (3 pc.)

85 Leaf Flower Bowl

94 Twin Ducks Planter (large size)

95 Twin Ducks Planter
(medium size)

144

Hull Pottery Co. CROOKSVILLE, OHIO

110 Clover Shaped Vase

60 Parrot with Cart Planter

113 Handled Planter Basket

88 Pup with Yarn Planter

111 Novelty Window Box

124 Rectangular Flower Dish

69 Swan Center Piece

80 Swan Planter

103 Twin Horn Vase

70 Swan Ash Tray or Planter

122 Handled Basket

61 Pheasant Planter

117 Oval Flower Bowl

118 Deep Oval Flower Bowl

Hull Pottery Co. CROOKSVILLE, OHIO

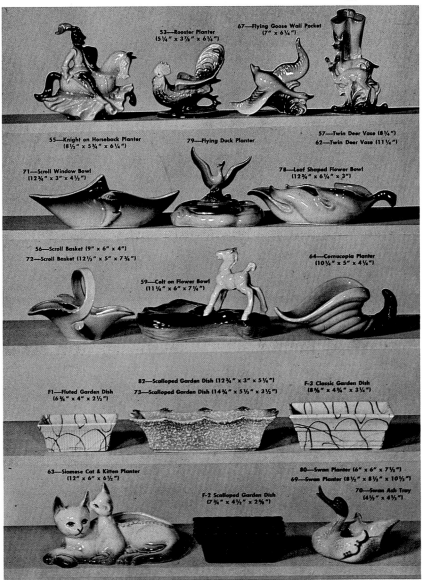

53—Rooster Planter
(5¼" x 3⅞" x 6¼")

67—Flying Goose Wall Pocket
(7" x 6¼")

55—Knight on Horseback Planter
(8½" x 5¾" x 6¼")

79—Flying Duck Planter

57—Twin Deer Vase (8¼")
62—Twin Deer Vase (11¼")

71—Scroll Window Bowl
(12¾" x 3" x 4½")

78—Leaf Shaped Flower Bowl
(12¾" x 6¼" x 3")

56—Scroll Basket (9" x 6" x 4")
72—Scroll Basket (12½" x 5" x 7¾")

59—Colt on Flower Bowl
(11¼" x 6" x 7¼")

64—Cornucopia Planter
(10¼" x 5" x 4¼")

F1—Fluted Garden Dish
(6¾" x 4" x 2½")

82—Scalloped Garden Dish (12¾" x 3" x 5¼")
73—Scalloped Garden Dish (14¾" x 5½" x 3½")

F-3 Classic Garden Dish
(8½" x 4¾" x 3¼")

63—Siamese Cat & Kitten Planter
(12" x 6" x 6½")

F-2 Scalloped Garden Dish
(7¾" x 4½" x 2⅝")

80—Swan Planter (6" x 6" x 7½")
69—Swan Planter (8½" x 8½" x 10½")

70—Swan Ash Tray
(4½" x 4½")

116—Printed in U. S. A.

146

HULL POTTERY CO. *Crooksville, Ohio*

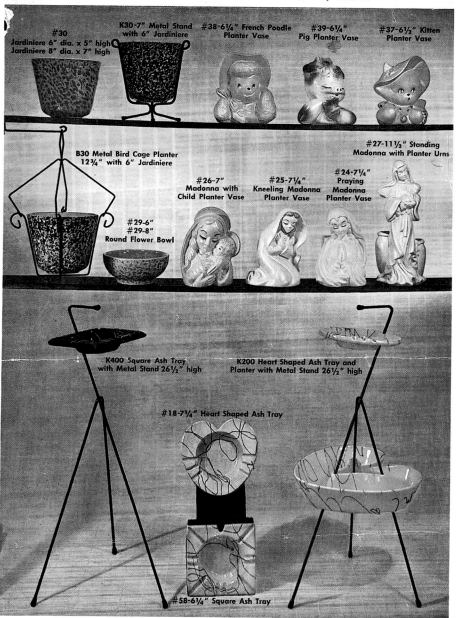

#30
Jardiniere 6" dia. x 5" high
Jardiniere 8" dia. x 7" high

K30-7" Metal Stand
with 6" Jardiniere

#38-6¼" French Poodle
Planter Vase

#39-6¼"
Pig Planter Vase

#37-6½" Kitten
Planter Vase

B30 Metal Bird Cage Planter
12¾" with 6" Jardiniere

#27-11½" Standing
Madonna with Planter Urns

#26-7"
Madonna with
Child Planter Vase

#25-7¼"
Kneeling Madonna
Planter Vase

#24-7¼"
Praying
Madonna
Planter Vase

#29-6"
#29-8"
Round Flower Bowl

K400 Square Ash Tray
with Metal Stand 26½" high

K200 Heart Shaped Ash Tray and
Planter with Metal Stand 26½" high

#18-7¼" Heart Shaped Ash Tray

#58-6¼" Square Ash Tray

147

W27—Creamer   W26—8 Cup Teapot   W28—Covered Sugar

W10—11" Cornucopia   30—8" Jardiniere   75—7" Jardiniere

65—5¾" Urn-Vase   93—6" Love Birds Planter   91—6¼" Fan Tailed Pigeon Planter

W22—10½" Handled Basket   W24—13½" Pitcher Vase   89—11½" St. Francis Planter

Hull 1

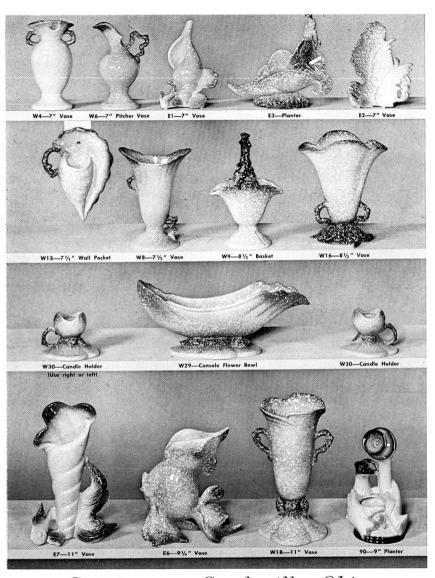

W4—7" Vase   W6—7" Pitcher Vase   E1—7" Vase   E3—Planter   E2—7" Vase

W13—7½" Wall Pocket   W8—7½" Vase   W9—8½" Basket   W16—8½" Vase

W30—Candle Holder (Use right or left)   W29—Console Flower Bowl   W30—Candle Holder

E7—11" Vase   E6—9¼" Vase   W18—11" Vase   90—9" Planter

ottery Company - - Crooksville, Ohio

150

Hull Pottery Company

W4—7" Vase W6—7" Vase E7—11" Vase W13—7½" Wall Pocket

W24—13½" Pitcher Vase W22—10½" Handled Basket W18—11" Vase

W9—8½" Basket W16—8½" Vase 65—5¾" Urn-Vase W10—11" Cornucopia

Hull Pottery Company

86-87—16½" Lavabo Set; Metal Hanging Rack

75—7" Jardiniere

75—6" Jardiniere

M30—Jardiniere (8"); Metal Stand (15" high)

N75—2 Jardinieres (6"); Metal Stand (16" high)

K200 Ash Tray and Planter with Metal Stand 26½" high

 *Athena* By HULL

Reflecting the classic beauty and perfect proportions of Greek architecture, this gracious ware is aptly named for Pallas Athena, goddess of peacetime industry. The fluted shapes, the graceful pedestals, the scrolled details were inspired by the Ionic, Doric and Corinthian columns of ancient Greece. Made in two decorations: Lilac trimmed in underglaze White Lava or Spring Green trimmed in underglaze White Lava. These are pieces especially designed to enhance floral arrangements and are in the best of taste.

601—Fluted Square Low
Flower Bowl
5¾"x5¾"x2¼"

Colors may be assorted as wanted

602—Free Form Low
Flower Bowl
8¾"x5½"x2¾"

603—Scroll Window Box
13"x4¼"x3¼"

604—Fluted Window Box
on Pedestal
9¾"x4"x5"

605—Flared Window Box
on Pedestal
11"x4½"x6"

*606—Ruffled Round
Planter on Pedestal
7" dia.x 6¼"

607—Paneled Square
Planter on Pedestal
5¾"x5¾"x6¼"

608—Cornucopia Vase
8½"

609—Ruffled Vase
on Pedestal
9" x 7"

610—Fan Vase
9" Hi. x 9" Wide

611—Oval Picture Frame
Wall Pocket Planter
8¼" Hi. x 6½" Wide

*Note: No's 606 and 607 may be assorted as wanted in the one dozen carton.

 Hull Pottery Company -- Crooksville, Ohio

153

FIESTA ART LINE DECORATIVE POTTERY

47
Fancy Jardiniere on Pedestal
with Embossed Berries on side
6½" x 6½"

48
Colonial Pitcher Vase
with Butterfly Embossing
8¾"

49
Fancy Italian Cornucopia
with Embossed Fruit
8½"

50
Fan Shape Vase
Embossed with Persian Gazelle
9½"

51
Planter Basket with Handle
Wicker and Leaf Embossing
12½" x 7"

52
Fancy Garden Dish Planter
with Wicker and Leaf Embossing
12½"

HULL POTTERY CO., Crooksville, Ohio

FIESTA ART LINE DECORATIVE POTTERY

40
Fancy Flower Pot
4 ¼" x 5 ¼"

41
Boat Shape Flower Bowl
on Pedestal
11" x 4 ¼"

42
Candle Holders
to match item #41
2 ¾" x 4 ½"

41/42 Three-piece Console Set

43
Footed Jardiniere
with Embossed Rose
6" x 5"

44
Duo-Tone Basket
with Handle
7" x 6 ½"

45
Footed Vase
with Embossed Strawberries
8 ½"

46
Footed Tulip Shape Jardiniere
with Embossed Strawberries
6 ½" x 5"

HULL POTTERY CO., Crooksville, Ohio

FIESTA

40
Fancy Flower Pot
4¼" x 5¼"

41
Boat Shape Flower Bowl
on Pedestal
11" x 4¼"

42
Candle Holders
to match item #41
2¾" x 4½"

43
Footed Jardiniere
with Embossed Rose
6" x 5"

44
Duo-Tone Basket
with Handle
7" x 6½"

45
Footed Vase
with Embossed Strawberries
8½"

46
Footed Tulip Shape Jardiniere
with Embossed Strawberries
6½" x 5"

47
Fancy Jardiniere on Pedestal
with Embossed Berries on side
6½" x 6½"

48
Colonial Pitcher Vase
with Butterfly Embossing
8¾"

HULL POTTERY COMPA

49
Fancy Italian Cornucopia
with Embossed Fruit
8½"

50
Fan Shape Vase
Embossed with Persian Gazelle
9½"

G10
Brass Table Stand
with 1 only #54, 5½" Dome Shape Pot
6½" High Overall

51
Planter Basket with Handle
Wicker and Leaf Embossing
12½" x 7"

52
Fancy Garden Dish Planter
with Wicker and Leaf Embossing
12½"

G9
Brass Floor Stand
with 1 only #53, 11" Jardiniere
21¼" High Overall

IY, Crooksville, Ohio

157

FIESTA *By* HULL

40
Fancy Flower Pot
4¼" x 5¼"

43
Footed Jardiniere
with Embossed Rose
6" x 5"

45
Footed Vase
with Embossed Strawberries
8½"

46
Footed Tulip Shape Jardiniere
with Embossed Strawberries
6½" x 5"

47
Fancy Jardiniere on Pedestal
with Embossed Berries on side
6½" x 6½"

48
Colonial Pitcher Vase
with Butterfly Embossing
8¾"

49
Fancy Italian Cornucopia
with Embossed Fruit
8½"

52
Fancy Garden Dish Planter
with Wicker and Leaf Embossing
12½"

50
Fan Shape Vase
Embossed with Persian Gazelle
9½"

HULL POTTERY COMPANY, Crooks

158

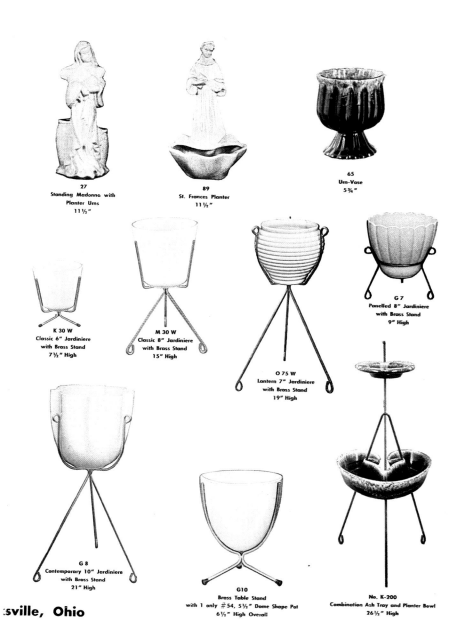

27
Standing Madonna with
Planter Urns
11½"

89
St. Frances Planter
11½"

65
Urn-Vase
5¾"

K 30 W
Classic 6" Jardiniere
with Brass Stand
7½" High

M 30 W
Classic 8" Jardiniere
with Brass Stand
15" High

O 75 W
Lantern 7" Jardiniere
with Brass Stand
19" High

G 7
Panelled 8" Jardiniere
with Brass Stand
9" High

G 8
Contemporary 10" Jardiniere
with Brass Stand
21" High

G10
Brass Table Stand
with 1 only #54, 5½" Dome Shape Pot
6½" High Overall

No. K-200
Combination Ash Tray and Planter Bowl
26½" High

:sville, Ohio

No. 49—Fancy Cornucopia
8½"

No. 50—Fan Shape Vase
9½"

No. 52—Garden Dish Planter
12½"

No. G9—Brass Stand with 11" Jardiniere
21" high

No. G10—Brass Stand with 5½" Pot
6½" high

Crooksville, Ohio

No. 101—Urn Vase 8"

No. 102—Footed Vase 11"

No. 103—Egyptian Vase 12"

A-900 Set

No. K-200
Combination Ash Tray and Planter Bowl
26½" High

HULL POTTERY COMPANY   **Crooksville, Ohio**

40
Fancy Flower Pot
4¼" x 5¼"

65
Urn-Vase
5¾"

No. 34
Scalloped Garden Dish
6½"x4"x2½"

No. 74
Window Box with Scalloped Top
13"x4¼"x3"

No. 37
Chinese Vase
8"

No. 71
Flower Arranger Vase
9"

No. 72
Footed Urn Vase
8½"

No. 39
Egyptian Vase
12"

45
Footed Vase
with Embossed Strawberries
8½"

46
Footed Tulip Shape Jardiniere
with Embossed Strawberries
6½" x 5"

HULL POTTERY COMPAI

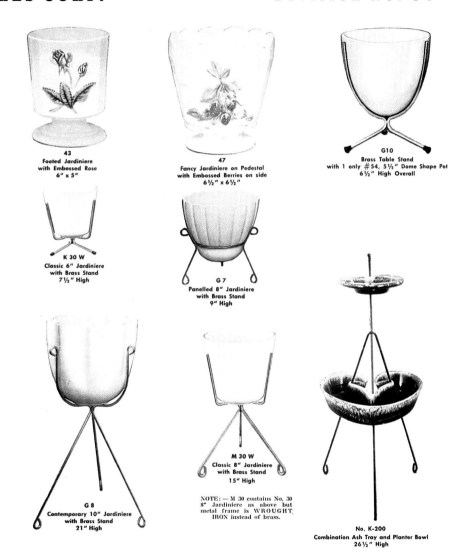

43
Footed Jardiniere
with Embossed Rose
6" x 5"

47
Fancy Jardiniere on Pedestal
with Embossed Berries on side
6½" x 6½"

G10
Brass Table Stand
with 1 only #54, 5½" Dome Shape Pot
6½" High Overall

K 30 W
Classic 6" Jardiniere
with Brass Stand
7½" High

G 7
Panelled 8" Jardiniere
with Brass Stand
9" High

M 30 W
Classic 8" Jardiniere
with Brass Stand
15" High

NOTE: — M 30 contains No. 30
8" Jardiniere as above but
metal frame is WROUGHT
IRON instead of brass.

G 8
Contemporary 10" Jardiniere
with Brass Stand
21" High

No. K-200
Combination Ash Tray and Planter Bowl
26½" High

Y, Crooksville, Ohio

#150—Crimped Top Flower Pot
3½" x 4¾"
Packed 1 dozen to carton
Weight 10 lbs.
Cost $3.00 per dozen
Retail Price 49c each

#149—Quilted Flower Pot
4" x 5¼"
Packed 1 dozen to carton
Weight 12 lbs.
Cost $4.56 per dozen
Retail Price 69c each

#31—Three Compartment Leaf Tray
9" x 7¾" x 1½"
Packed 1 dozen to carton
Weight 15 lbs.
Cost $4.80 per dozen
Retail Price 79c each

Sun Valley Pastels
by HULL

ELEVEN ITEMS IN CHOICE of
M1—Satin Pink outside, Gloss Gray inside
M2—Satin Turquoise outside, Gloss Yellow inside

#158—Pedestaled Square Planter
4¾" x 5½"
Packed 1 dozen to carton
Weight 18 lbs.
Cost $7.20 per dozen
Retail Price $1.19 each

#157—Pedestaled Rectangular Dish
7" x 5" x 4"
Packed ½ dozen to carton
Weight 11 lbs.
Cost $7.80 per dozen
Retail Price $1.19 each

#156—Pedestaled Octagonal Planter
4⅞" x 5¾"
Packed 1 dozen to carton
Weight 12 lbs.
Cost $6.60 per dozen
Retail Price 98c each

#158C—Pedestaled Square Candy Dish w/Cover
6⅞"
Packed 1 dozen to carton
Weight 24 lbs.
Cost $9.60 per dozen
Retail Price $1.49 each

#155—Rectangular Planter
12" x 6½" x 3½"
Packed ½ dozen to carton
Weight 17 lbs.
Cost $11.76 per dozen
Retail Price $1.89 each

#159—Footed Compote
10½" Diameter x 5¼" High
Packed 1/3 dozen to carton
Weight 16 lbs.
Cost $13.50 per dozen
Retail Price $1.98 each

Hull Pottery Co.

716—Printed in U. S. A.

Terms: 1% 15. Net 30.   F. O. B. Factory at Crooksville. No Package Charge.

164

#153—Window Box
13" x 4¼" x 3"
Packed 2/3 dozen to carton
Weight 18 lbs.
Cost $6.60 per dozen
Retail Price 98c

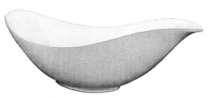

#152—Modern Flower Dish
12¾" x 5¼"
Packed 2/3 dozen to carton
Weight 15 lbs.
Cost $8.16 per dozen
Retail Price $1.29 each

SEVEN ITEMS IN CHOICE of
M3—Satin Pink outside, Gloss inside
M4—Satin Willow Green outside, Gloss inside
M5—Satin White outside, Gloss inside
NOTE—No. 154 in two sizes

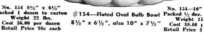

#151—Modern Flower Dish
13" x 4¾"
Packed 2/3 dozen to carton
Weight 12 lbs.
Cost $6.60 per dozen
Retail Price 98c each

No. 154 8½" x 6½"
Packed 1 dozen to carton
Weight 22 lbs.
Cost $6.00 per dozen
Retail Price 98c each

#154—Fluted Oval Bulb Bowl
8½" x 6½", also 10" x 7½"

No. 154—10"
Packed ½ doz.
Weight 15
Cost $8.40
Retail Price $

#160—Cylindrical Vase
9"
Packed ½ dozen to carton
Weight 12 lbs.
Cost $6.36 per dozen
Retail Price 98c each

#161—Urn Vase
8¼"
Packed ½ dozen to carton
Weight 16½ lbs.
Cost $6.60 per dozen
Retail Price 98c each

#162—Tulip Vase
11¾"
Packed ½ dozen to carton
Weight 16 lbs.
Cost $13.20 per dozen
Retail Price $1.98 each

#163—Flared Top Vase
11½"
Packed ½ dozen to carton
Weight 16 lbs.
Cost $13.20 per dozen
Retail Price $1.98 each

Company :: Crooksville, Ohio

(See Over for 66 Piece Introductory Assortment On Above Items

C M S FANTASY

No. 74
Window Box with Scalloped Top
13"x4¼"x3"

No. 38
Pedestaled Square Planter
4¾"x5½"

No. 76
Pedestaled Urn Jardiniere
6½"x5½"

No. 79
Footed Round Planter Bowl
6½"x5½"

No. 90
Cherub Planter
9"x7¼"

No. 79C
Footed Candy Dish and Cover with Brass Knob
8¼"x6½"

No. 77
Oval Footed Compote Flower Bowl
11½"x7½

Nos. 77-78
3-Pc. Compote Console Set

No. 78
Candle Stick (to match No. 77)
6½"

HULL POTTERY COMPANY, Crooksville, Ohio

166

C M S   FANTASY

No. 71
Flower Arranger Vase
9"

No. 37
Chinese Vase
8"

No. 72
Footed Urn Vase
8½"

No. 73
Footed Vase with Scalloped Top
10"

No. 39
Egyptian Vase
12"

No. 34
Scalloped Garden Dish
6½"x4"x2½"

No. 35
Modern Garden Dish
8½"x5"x3"

No. 36
Victorian Flower Bowl
9¼"x3¾"x4"

HULL POTTERY COMPANY, Crooksville, Ohio

BASIC LIST ILLUSTRATION **REGIONS** 1-2-3-4 (Planter Bar Stores) **EFFECTIVE DATE** April 1958 **DEPT.** 89 **PAGE NO.** 2545 A

ORDERING INFORMATION
ON BASIC LIST PAGE NOS. See following pages

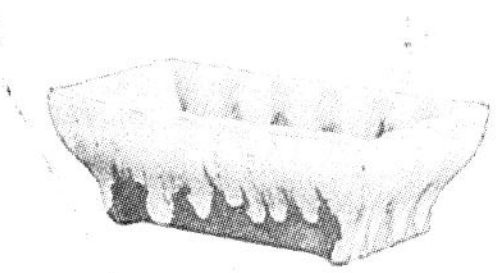

No. 6379
Scalloped Garden Dish
6½"x4"x2½"

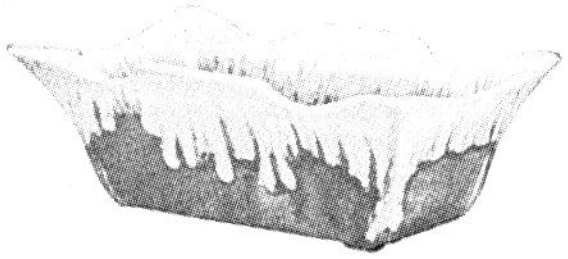

No. 6380
Modern Garden Dish
8½"x5"x3"

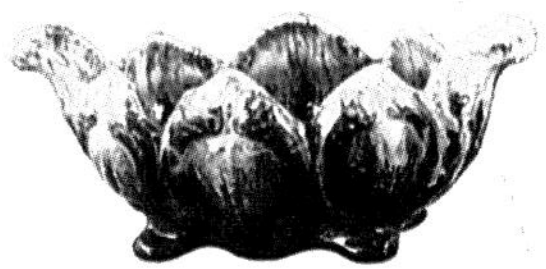

No. 6381
Victorian Flower Bowl
9¼"x3¾"x4"

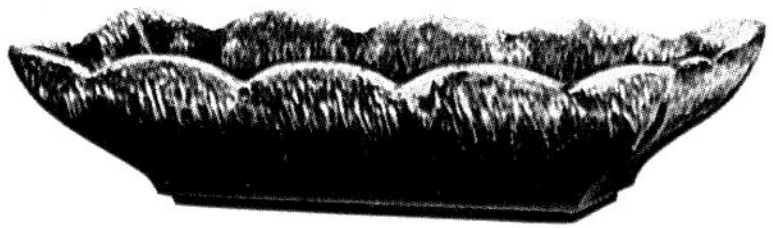

No. 6382
Window Box with Scalloped Top
13"x4¼"x3"

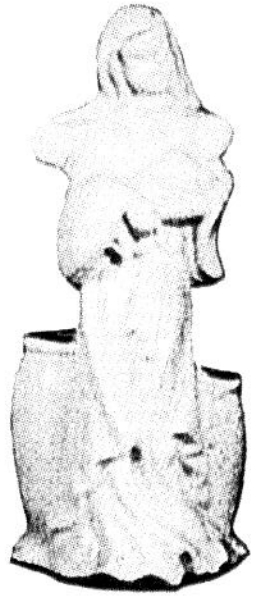

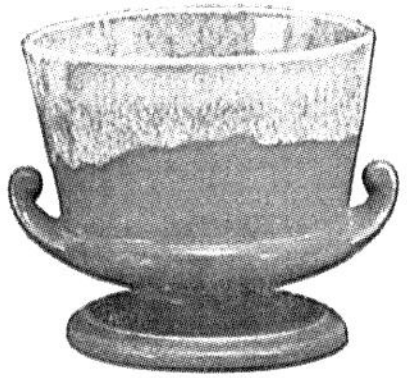

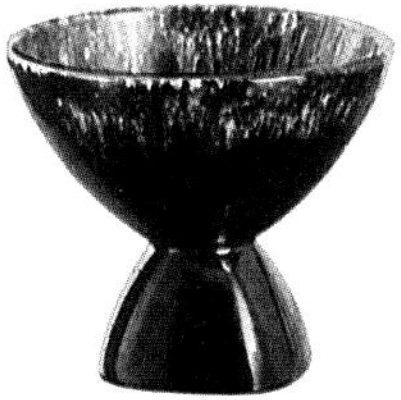

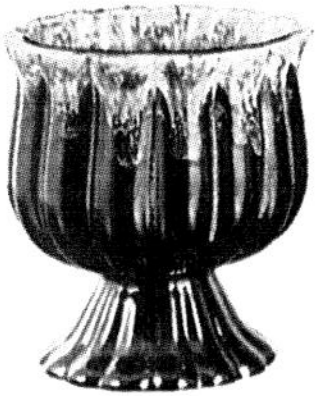

No. 6385
Standing Madonna with
Planter Urns
11½"

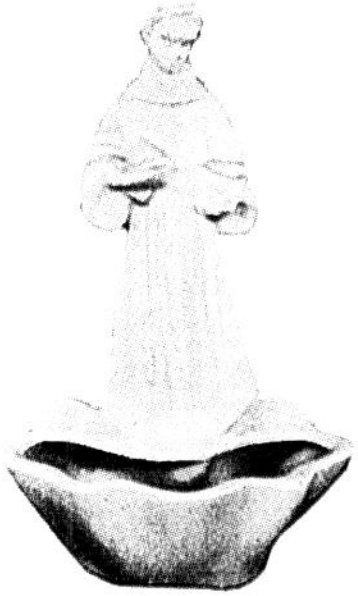

No. 6386
St. Frances Planter
11½"

No. 6383
Pedestaled Urn Jardiniere
6½"x5½"

No. 6384
Footed Round Planter Bowl
6½"x5½"

No. 6387
Urn-Vase
5¾"

28741-3

REPLACES PAGE NO. DATED **PAGE NO.** 2545 A

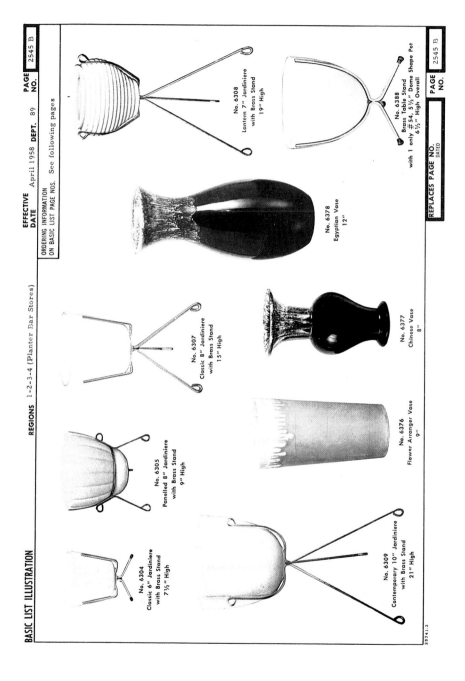

No. 6308
Lantern 7" Jardiniere
with Brass Stand
19" High

No. 6388
Brass Table Stand
with 1 only # 54, 5½" Dome Shape Pot
6½" High Overall

No. 6378
Egyptian Vase
12"

No. 6307
Classic 8" Jardiniere
with Brass Stand
15" High

No. 6377
Chinese Vase
8"

No. 6376
Flower Arranger Vase
9"

No. 6305
Panelled 8" Jardiniere
with Brass Stand
9" High

No. 6304
Classic 6" Jardiniere
with Brass Stand
7½" High

No. 6309
Contemporary 10" Jardiniere
with Brass Stand
21" High

ORDERING INFORMATION
ON BASIC LIST PAGE NOS. See following pages

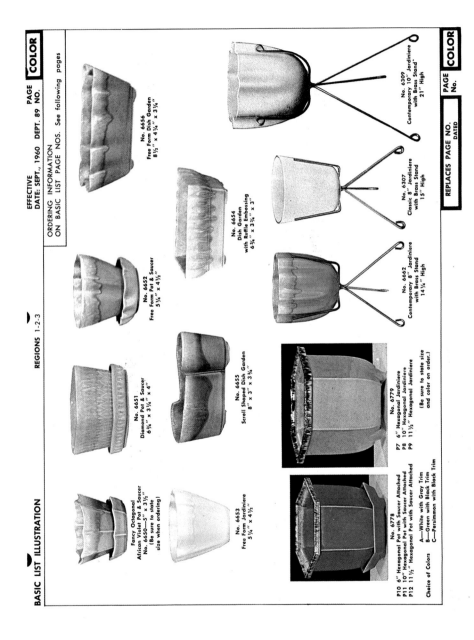

No. 6656
Free Form Dish Garden
8½″ x 4¾″ x 3¼″

No. 6654
Dish Garden
with Ruffle Embossing
6¾″ x 3¾″ x 3″

No. 6652
Free Form Pot & Saucer
5¼″ x 4½″

No. 6651
Diamond Pot & Saucer
6¾″ x 3¼″ x 4″

No. 6655
Scroll Shaped Dish Garden
8″ x 3″ x 3¾″

Fancy Octagonal
African Violet Pot & Saucer
No. 6650—5″ x 3½″
(Be sure to state
size when ordering)

No. 6653
Free Form Jardiniere
5¼″ x 4½″

No. 6309
Contemporary 10″ Jardiniere
with Brass Stand
21″ High

No. 6307
Classic 8″ Jardiniere
with Brass Stand
15″ High

No. 6662
Contemporary 6″ Jardiniere
with Brass Stand
14¼″ High

No. 6778
P10 6″ Hexagonal Pot with Saucer Attached
P11 10″ Hexagonal Pot with Saucer Attached
P12 11½″ Hexagonal Pot with Saucer Attached

Choice of Colors
A—White with Gray Trim
B—Green with Black Trim
C—Persimmon with Black Trim

No. 6779
P7 6″ Hexagonal Jardiniere
P8 10″ Hexagonal Jardiniere
P9 11½″ Hexagonal Jardiniere
(Be sure to state size
and color on order.)

REPLACES PAGE NO. PAGE No. COLOR
DATED

170

BASIC LIST ILLUSTRATION

REGIONS 1-2-3

EFFECTIVE
DATE: SEPT., 1960   DEPT. 89 NO.

PAGE
NO.

COLOR

ORDERING INFORMATION
ON BASIC LIST PAGE NOS. See following pages

No. 6660
Swan Centerpiece
or Planter
7½" x 9" x 10"

No. 6752—10"
Cornucopia Planter

No. 6751—7" Scalloped
Compote Bowl

No. 6750—6¾" Pedestaled
Free Form Flower Bowl

No. 6382
Window Box with Scalloped Top
13" x 4¼" x 3"

No. 6387
Urn-Vase
5¾"

No. 6754—10" x 4¼" Oval
Flower Bowl

No. 6753—7¼" x 2¾"
Scalloped Low Flower Bowl

PLANTERS

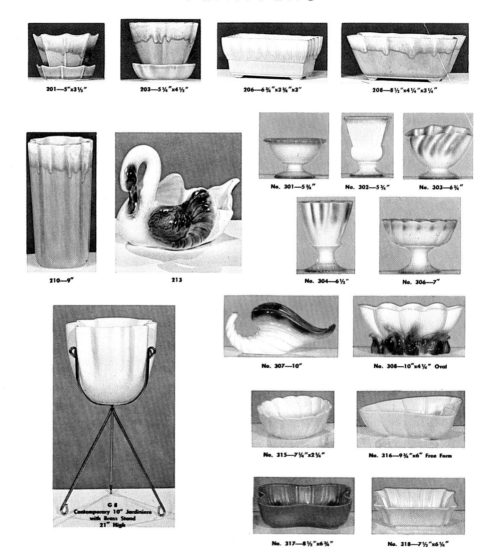

201—5"x3½"

203—5¼"x4½"

206—6¾"x3¾"x3"

208—8½"x4¼"x3¼"

210—9"

213

No. 301—5¾"

No. 302—5¾"

No. 303—6¾"

No. 304—6½"

No. 306—7"

No. 307—10"

No. 308—10"x4¼" Oval

No. 315—7¼"x2¼"

No. 316—9¾"x6" Free Form

No. 317—8½"x6¾"

No. 318—7½"x6¼"

G 8
Contemporary 10" Jardiniere
with Brass Stand
21" High

Hull Pottery Company - - Crooksville, Ohio

172

No. 301—5¾" Pedestaled Round Flower Bowl   No. 302—5¾" Square Top Urn Vase   No. 303—6¾" Pedestaled Free Form Flower Bowl   No. 304—6½" Chalice Planter/Vase   No. 305—6½" Butterfly Flower Bowl on Pedestal   No. 306—7" Scalloped Compote Bowl

No. 307—10" Cornucopia Planter   No. 308—10" x 4¼" Oval Flower Bowl   No. 309—9" Flamingo Vase   No. 310—11" Flying Duck Vase

No. 311—11" Unicorn Vase   No. 312—13" Twin Deer Vase   No. 313—12¼" x 7½" x 5¼" Parrot Planter   No. 314—10½" x 8" Flying Duck Planter

No. 315—7¼" x 2¼" Scalloped Low Flower Bowl   No. 316—9¾" x 6" Free Form Low Flower Bowl   No. 317—8½" x 6¾" Contemporary Low Flower Bowl   No. 318—7½" x 6¼" Oriental Low Flower Bowl

 Hull Pottery Company - - Crooksville, Ohio

ORDERING INFORMATION
ON BASIC LIST PAGE Nos. See following pages

P3, P4, P5, & P6 are Available
in the following colors.

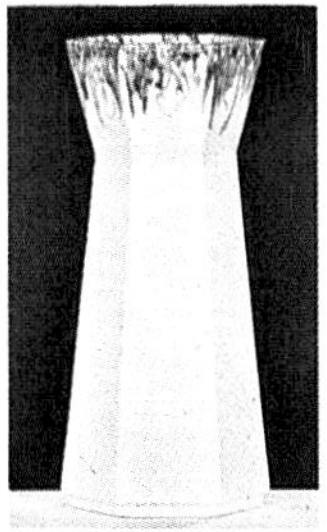

A—White with Gray Trim
B—Green with Black Trim
C—Persimmon with Black Trim

(Be sure to state size and color
when ordering).

P 3
7½" Hexagonal Vase

P 4
10" Hexagonal Vase

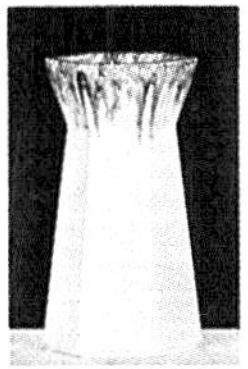

P 5
12" Hexagonal Vase

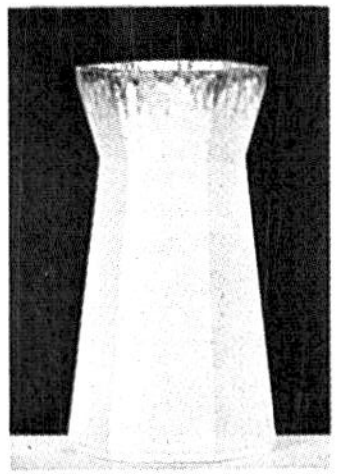

P 6
15" Hexagonal Vase

No. 312—13"
Twin Deer Vase

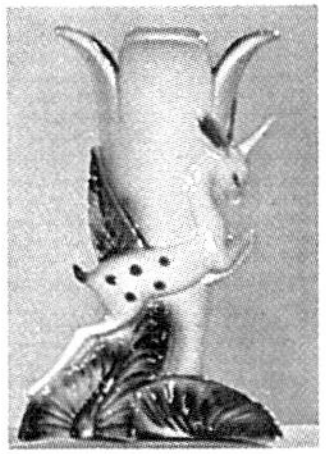

No. 311—11"
Unicorn Vase

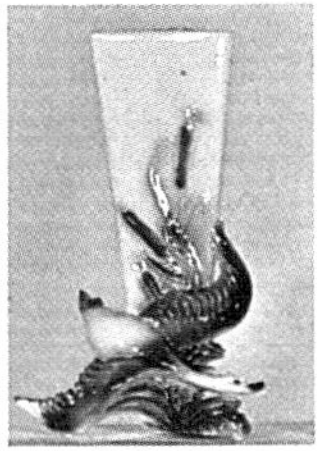

No. 310—11"
Flying Duck Vase

No. 309—9"
Flamingo Vase

Regal

Dept. 24

No. 301—5¾" Pedestaled
Round Flower Bowl

No. 302—5¾"
Square Top Urn Vase

No. 304—6½"
Chalice Planter/Vase

No. 305—6½" Butterfly
Flower Bowl on Pedestal

No. 306—7" Scalloped
Compote Bowl

No. 303—6¾" Pedestaled
Free Form Flower Bowl
Plant Not Included

No. 307—10"
Cornucopia Planter

No. 308—10" x 4¼" Oval
Flower Bowl

No. 309—9"
Flamingo Vase

No. 310—11"
Flying Duck Vase

No. 313—12¼" x 7½" x 5¼"
Parrot Planter

No. 314—10½" x 8"
Flying Duck Planter

No. 311—11"
Unicorn Vase

No. 312—13"
Twin Deer Vase

No. 315—7¼" x 2¼"
Scalloped Low Flower Bowl

No. 316—9¾" x 6" Free Form
Low Flower Bowl

No. 317—8½" x 6¾"
Contemporary Low Flower Bowl

No. 318—7½" x 6¼"
Oriental Low Flower Bowl

HULL POTTERY COMPANY

Crooksville, Ohio

HULL

Casual Set
Smoker and Planter

Wrought-iron stand 24" high holds decorated 11¼" pottery ash tray and 5" planter, both removable. Planter may be used for smoking supplies. Your choice of:

    A—Pink with Black trim.
    B—Milk White with Gray trim.
    D—Green with Black trim.

A-900 Set

A-5 Ash Tray   204 Planter

A-5 Ash Tray   204 Planter

 Hull Pottery Company - - Crooksville, Ohio

176

Coronet By HULL

201—5"x3½" also 201—5½"x4"	202—6¾"x3¼"x4"	203—5¼"x4½"	204—5¼"
206—6¾"x3¾"x3"	207—8"x3"x3¾"	208—8½"x4¼"x3¼"	
205B 14¼" Overall High	209—9"	210—9"	211—10½"
	212	213	

HULL POTTERY COMPANY, Crooksville, Ohio

Jubilee by HULL

401
Scalloped Garden Dish
6 ¼" x 4" x 2 ½"

403
Victorian Flower Bowl
9 ¼" x 4 ¾" x 4"

402
Modern Garden Dish
8 ½" x 5" x 3"

427
Contemporary Jardiniere
10" Diameter

426
Classic Panelled Jardiniere
8" Diameter

421
Embossed Italian Footed Vase
11 ½" High

K 30 W
Classic 6" Jardiniere
with Brass Stand
7 ½" High

M 30 W
Classic 8" Jardiniere
with Brass Stand
15" High

O 75 W
Lantern 7" Jardiniere
with Brass Stand
19" High

G 8
Contemporary 10" Jardiniere
with Brass Stand
21" High

THE HULL POTTERY COMPANY, Crooksville, Ohio

Jubilee *by* HULL

411	412	413	418
"The Duchess" Planter	"The Duchess" Ash Tray	Swan Table Planter	Top Hat Basket
12¼" High	5¼" High	10½" High	8¾" High

404
Free-Form Window Box
13½" x 5½" x 2½"

405
Caladium Leaf Flower Bowl
13½" x 10¾"

401
Scalloped Garden Dish
6¼" x 4" x 2½"

402
Modern Garden Dish
8½" x 5" x 3"

403
Victorian Flower Bowl
9¼" x 4¾" x 4"

HULL POTTERY COMPANY   **CROOKSVILLE, OHIO**

Printed in U. S. A.

Jubilee by HULL

K 500 B
Ash Tray and Planter
with Brass Stand
26½" High

G 8
Contemporary 10" Jardiniere
with Brass Stand
21" High

O 75 W
Lantern 7" Jardiniere
with Brass Stand
19" High

G6-425
Embossed 4½" Jardiniere
with Brass Stand
5½" High

G6-150
Crimped 3½" Flower Pot
with Brass Stand
4½" High

M 30 W
Classic 8" Jardiniere
with Brass Stand
15" High

G 7
Panelled 8" Jardiniere
with Brass Stand
9" High

K 30 W
Classic 6" Jardiniere
with Brass Stand
7½" High

HULL POTTERY COMPANY · **CROOKSVILLE, OHIO**

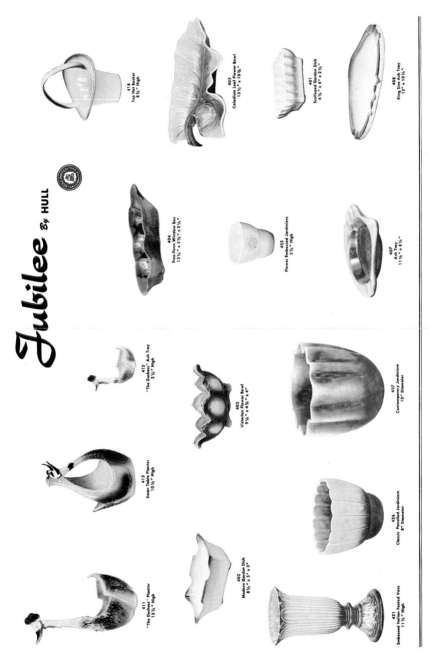

Jubilee By HULL

418
Top Hat Basket
8½" High

405
Caladium Leaf Flower Bowl
13½" x 10¾"

401
Scalloped Garden Dish
6¼" x 4" x 2½"

408
King Size Ash Tray
13" x 10½"

404
Free-Form Window Box
13½" x 5½" x 2½"

425
Flower Embossed Jardiniere
5½" High

407
Ash Tray
11½" x 8¼"

412
"The Duchess" Ash Tray
5¼" High

403
Victorian Flower Bowl
9¼" x 4½" x 4"

427
Contemporary Jardiniere
10" Diameter

413
Swan Table Planter
10½" High

426
Classic Panelled Jardiniere
8" Diameter

411
"The Duchess" Planter
13½" High

402
Modern Garden Dish
8½" x 5" x 3"

421
Embossed Italian Footed Vase
11½" High

THE HULL POTTERY COMPANY, Crooksville, Ohio

BASIC LIST ILLUSTRATION

REGIONS 1-2-3-4

EFFECTIVE DATE AUG. 1960

Dept. 86

PAGE NO.

COLOR

ORDERING INFORMATION
ON BASIC LIST PAGE Nos. See following pages

No. 103—Egyptian Vase 12"

No. 102—Footed Vase 11"

No. 101—Urn Vase 8"

Colors for 101—102—103
Milk White with Gold
Bands, Sage Green with
Gold Bands, Rancho Gold
with Gold Bands.

No. 211—Footed
Vase 10½"
Colors Yellow—Chartreuse
Gray—Turquoise

No. 210—Free Form
Vase 9¼"
Colors Yellow—Chartreuse
Gray—Turquoise

No. 112—Gladiolus Vase 10"
Colors Milk White & Jetblack

182

No. 206—6¾" x 3¼" x 3"

No. 207—8" x 3" x 3¾"

No. 208—8½" x 4¼" x 3¼"

No. 201—5"x3½" also 201—5½"x4"

No. 203—5¼"x4½"

No. 210—9"

No. 213

M 30 W
Classic 8" Jardiniere
with Brass Stand
15" High

G 8
Contemporary 10" Jardiniere
with Brass Stand
21" High

Hull Pottery Company - - Crooksville, Ohio

No. 301—5¾" Pedestaled
Round Flower Bowl

No. 302—5¾"
Square Top Urn Vase

No. 303—6¾" Pedestaled
Free Form Flower Bowl

No. 304—6½"
Chalice Planter/Vase

No. 306—7" Scalloped
Compote Bowl

No. 307—10"
Cornucopia Planter

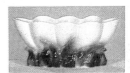

No. 308—10" x 4¼" Oval
Flower Bowl

No. 318—7½" x 6¼"
Oriental Low Flower Bowl

No. 316—9¾" x 6" Free Form
Low Flower Bowl

Hull Pottery Company - - Crooksville, Ohio

ROSE'S 5-10-25c STORES INC.

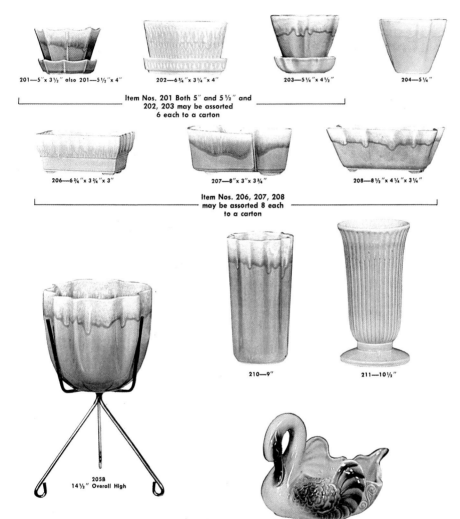

201—5″x 3½″ also 201—5½″x 4″

202—6¾″x 3¼″x 4″

203—5¼″x 4½″

204—5¼″

Item Nos. 201 Both 5″ and 5½″ and
202, 203 may be assorted
6 each to a carton

206—6¾″x 3¾″x 3″

207—8″x 3″x 3¾″

208—8½″x 4¼″x 3¼″

Item Nos. 206, 207, 208
may be assorted 8 each
to a carton

210—9″

211—10½″

205B
14½″ Overall High

213

ROSE'S 5-10-25c STORES INC.

No. 101—Urn Vase 8"

No. 102—Footed Vase 11"

No. 103—Egyptian Vase 12"

No. 105—Pedestaled Jardiniere 6"
(Pedestaled Jardiniere 7½"
and 10" Available But
Not Shown)

No. 105—Pedestaled
Jardiniere 8½"

No. 94B—5"
Bucket Jardiniere
Wood Embossed

No. 94B—6"
Bucket Jardiniere
Wood Embossed

No. 94B—7"
Bucket Jardiniere
Wood Embossed

G 8
Contemporary 10" Jardiniere
with Brass Stand
21" High

M 30
Wrought Iron
M 30 W Brass
Classic 8" Jardiniere
with Brass Stand
15" High

186

No. 206—6¾" x 3¾" x 3"

No. 207—8" x 3" x 3¾"

No. 208—8½" x 4¼" x 3¼"

No. 201—5"x3½" also 201—5½"x4"

No. 202—6¾"x3¼"x4"

No. 203—5¼"x4½"

No. 210—9"

No. 211—10½"

No. 213

Hull Pottery Company - - Crooksville, Ohio

187

H. L. GREEN CO.

No. 207

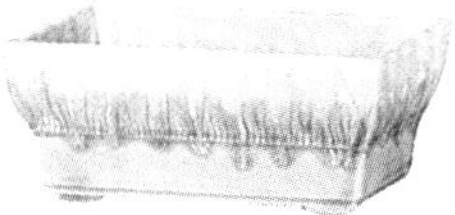

No. 206

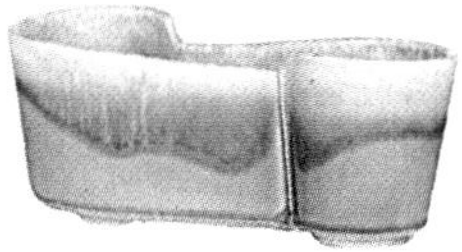

No. 203

No. 202

213

948—6"

948—5"

210—9"

212

209—9"

205B
14½" Overall High

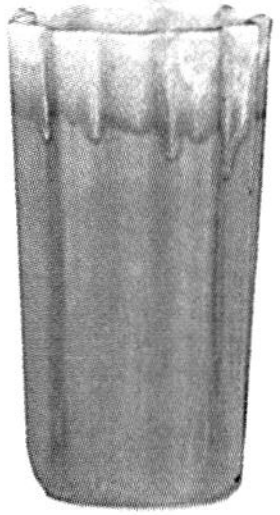

HULL POTTERY COMPANY, Crooksville, Ohio

188

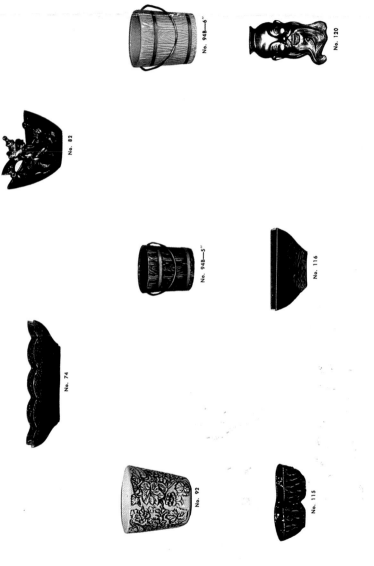

H. L. GREEN CO.

No. 82

No. 74

No. 92

No. 94B—6"

No. 120

No. 94B—5"

No. 116

No. 115

HULL POTTERY CO., Crooksville, Ohio

No. 101—Urn Vase 8"

No. 102—Footed Vase 11"

No. 103—Egyptian Vase 12"

No. 104—Modern Decorato Vase 15"

No. 105—Pedestaled Jardiniere 6"
(Pedestaled Jardinieres 7½"
and 10" Available But
Not Shown)

No. 105—Pedestaled
Jardiniere 8½"

No. 110—Unique Two Way
Footed Vase 10"
Candle and Flower not Included
(Reverses into Flower Vase)

No. 111—Graceful Slender Neck
Pitcher Vase 15"

No. 112—Gladiolus Vase 10"

No. 94B—5"
Bucket Jardiniere
Wood Embossed

No. 94B—6"
Bucket Jardiniere
Wood Embossed

HULL POTTERY CO

Gold-Medal Flowerware

By HULL

No. 115
Peanut Shaped Garden Dish
8" x 3¾" x 2¾"

No. 116
Wood Embossed Garden Dish
8½" x 5¼" x 3½"

No. 117—Round Flower Bowl
W/Wicker 9"

No. 118—Leaf Planter 11½"

No. 119—Classic Chinese
Unicorn Planter 9"

No. 120—Chinese Sage Mask
Wall Pocket 8"

No. 94B—7"
Bucket Jardiniere
Wood Embossed

No. 96B—8"
Tub Shaped Azalea
Jardiniere

No. 96B—10"
Tub Shaped Azalea
Jardiniere

OMPANY = = *Crooksville, Ohio*

191

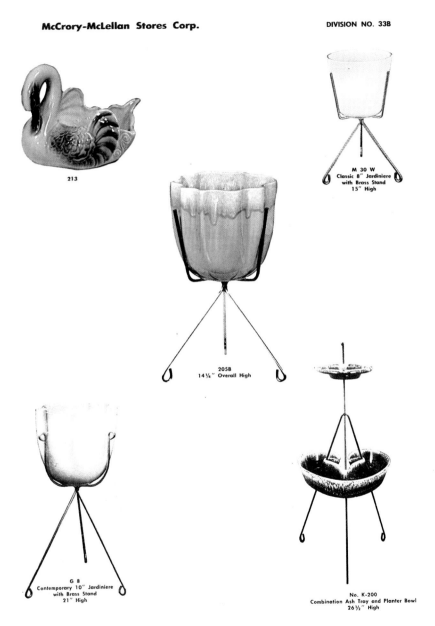

213

M 30 W
Classic 8" Jardiniere
with Brass Stand
15" High

205B
14¼" Overall High

G 8
Contemporary 10" Jardiniere
with Brass Stand
21" High

No. K-200
Combination Ash Tray and Planter Bowl
26½" High

HULL POTTERY COMPANY, Crooksville, Ohio

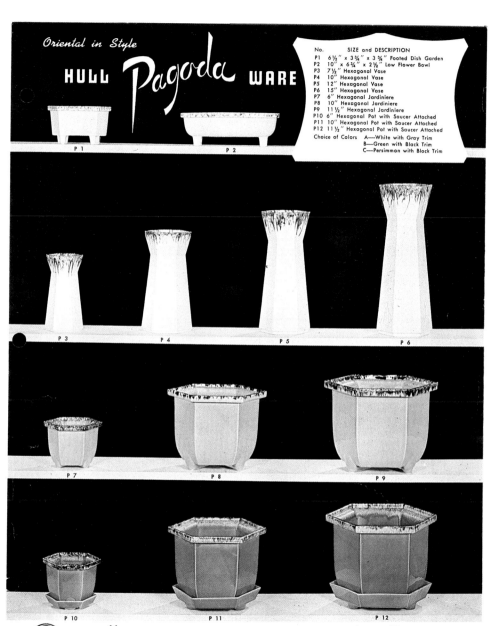

Oriental in Style

HULL *Pagoda* WARE

No.	SIZE and DESCRIPTION
P1	6½" x 3¾" x 3¾" Footed Dish Garden
P2	10" x 6¾" x 2½" Low Flower Bowl
P3	7½" Hexagonal Vase
P4	10" Hexagonal Vase
P5	12" Hexagonal Vase
P6	15" Hexagonal Vase
P7	6" Hexagonal Jardiniere
P8	10" Hexagonal Jardiniere
P9	11½" Hexagonal Jardiniere
P10	6" Hexagonal Pot with Saucer Attached
P11	10" Hexagonal Pot with Saucer Attached
P12	11½" Hexagonal Pot with Saucer Attached

Choice of Colors   A—White with Gray Trim
   B—Green with Black Trim
   C—Persimmon with Black Trim

P 1   P 2

P 3   P 4   P 5   P 6

P 7   P 8   P 9

P 10   P 11   P 12

Hull Pottery Company - - Crooksville, Ohio

201—5½" x 4"   202—6¾" x 3¼" x 4"   203—5¼" x 4½"

Assortment No. 360R consists of 8 each of the above 3 Pots and Saucers

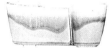

206—6¾" x 3¾" x 3"   208—8½" x 4¼" x 3¼"

Assortment No. 304R consists of 8 each of the above 3 Dish Gardens

210—9"   No. 101—Urn Vase 8"   110—10"

211—10½"

No. 102—Footed Vase 11"   No. 103—Egyptian Vase 12"

No. 104—Modern Decorator
Vase 15"

HULL POTTERY COMPANY, Crooksville, Ohio

No. 101—Urn Vase 8"

No. 102—Footed Vase 11"

No. 103—Egyptian Vase 12" ·

No. 104—Modern Decorator
Vase 15"

Gold-Medal Flowerware

By HULL

No. 110—Unique Two Way
Footed Vase 10"
Candle and Flower not Included
(Reverses into Flower Vase)

No. 111—Graceful Slender Neck
Pitcher Vase 15"

No. K-200
Combination Ash Tray and Planter Bowl
26½" High

HULL POTTERY COMPANY, Crooksville, Ohio

No. 105—Pedestaled Jardiniere 6"
(Pedestaled Jardinieres 7½"
and 10" Available But
Not Shown)

No. 105—Pedestaled
Jardiniere 8½"

94-B—HI-BUCKETS
Sizes—5" - 6" - 7" & 9"
(9" Not Shown)

No. 96B—8"
Tub Shaped Azalea
Jardiniere

No. 96B—10"
Tub Shaped Azalea
Jardiniere

Gold-Medal Flowerware

 By HULL

HULL POTTERY COMPANY, Crooksville, Ohio

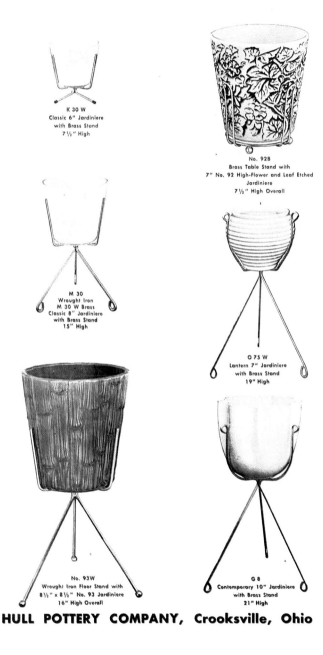

K 30 W
Classic 6" Jardiniere
with Brass Stand
7½" High

No. 92B
Brass Table Stand with
7" No. 92 High-Flower and Leaf Etched
Jardiniere
7½" High Overall

M 30
Wrought Iron
M 30 W Brass
Classic 8" Jardiniere
with Brass Stand
15" High

O 75 W
Lantern 7" Jardiniere
with Brass Stand
19" High

No. 93W
Wrought Iron Floor Stand with
8½" x 8½" No. 93 Jardiniere
16" High Overall

G 8
Contemporary 10" Jardiniere
with Brass Stand
21" High

HULL POTTERY COMPANY, Crooksville, Ohio

197

Medley

801—Urn Vase
5" Hi—3" opening

802—Urn Vase
6" Hi—4¼" opening

803—Urn Vase
7" Hi—5½" opening

804—Urn Vase
8" Hi—6" opening

805—Pedestaled
Flower Bowl 5"

806—Jardiniere
Three footed 5¾"x5"

807—Bell shaped Vase 9"

808—8" Twist Vase—
Hour-glass shape

**The following item is made in 3 decorations SATIN WHITE—GREEN AGATE w/TUR-
QUOISE STRIPE—PERSIMMON w/YELLOW STRIPE.

*The following items are made in 3 colors: SATIN WHITE—GREEN AGATE—PERSIMMON

**809—11" Cat Vase

*810—5¼"
Dolphin Flower Arranger

*811—Teddy Bear Planter
7½" x 6¾"

†The following item is made in 3 colors: SATIN
WHITE—GREEN AGATE—trimmed in TURQUOISE and
PERSIMMON trimmed in GREEN.

‡The following item is made in 3 colors: SATIN
WHITE—GREEN AGATE w/TURQUOISE FLOW—PER-
SIMMON w/GREEN FLOW.

†812—Swan & Planter
9" x 7½"

813—Madonna Planter
9" x 7½"
SATIN WHITE only

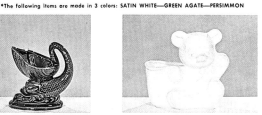

‡814—Low Flower Bowl
11½" x 5¼" x 3"

 Hull Pottery Company - - Crooksville, Ohio

FLOWER BOWLS and PLANTERS

F15—Oval Pedestaled Vase
5 ¾"x5 ½"

F44—Round Flower Bowl
4 ¼"x5 ¾"

F45—Ribbed Flower Bowl
4 ¼"x6"

303—Pedestaled Free Form
Flower Bowl 6 ¾"

318—Low Flower Bowl
7 ½"x6 ¼"

206—Dish Garden with Ruffle
Embossing 6 ¾"x3 ¾"x3"

208—Dish Garden
8 ½"x4 ¼"x3 ¼"

602—Free Form Flower Bowl
8 ¾"x5 ½"x2 ¾"

603—Scroll Window Box
13"x4 ¼"x3 ¼"

213—Swan Centerpiece or Planter
7 ½"x9"x10"
Color: MILK WHITE w/Green TRIM

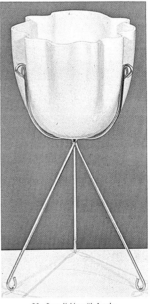

G8—Brass Holder with 1 only
#427—10 ½" Jard.
(21" Hi.) GREEN—BLACK—WHITE ENAMEL

 Hull Pottery Company - - Crooksville, Ohio

199

"*Supreme*"

No. 1 Bud Vase 8"

No. 2 Urn
5½" Dia. x 5¾" High

No. 3 Jardiniere
5¾" Dia. x 4½" High

No. 4 Footed Bowl
7½" Dia. x 4½" High

A—Agate & Chartreuse

No. 5 Basket 8¾"

No. 6 Candy Box
6¼" Dia. x 7" High

No. 7 Pedestal Vase 10"

No. 8 Jug
5¼" Dia. x 9½" High

No. 9 Exotic Vase 12¼"

200

Sculptured Designs by *Louise*

No. 1 Bud Vase 8"

No. 2 Urn
5½" Dia. x 5¾" High

No. 3 Jardiniere
5¾" Dia. x 4½" High

No. 4 Footed Bowl
7½" Dia. x 4½" High

B—Ripe Olive & Orange

No. 5 Basket 8¾"

No. 6 Candy Box
6¼" Dia. x 7" High

No. 7 Pedestal Vase 10"

No. 8 Jug
5½" Dia. x 9½" High

No. 9 Exotic Vase 12¼"

hull pottery company—crooksville, ohio 43731

Page 1—See page 1 in Price List

Decoration: #1 — Satin White #3 — Turquoise w/White Flow
#2 — Moss Green #4 — Coral w/White Flow
#5 — Mahogany w/White Flow

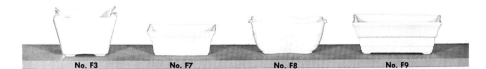

Imperial — made especially for FLORISTS

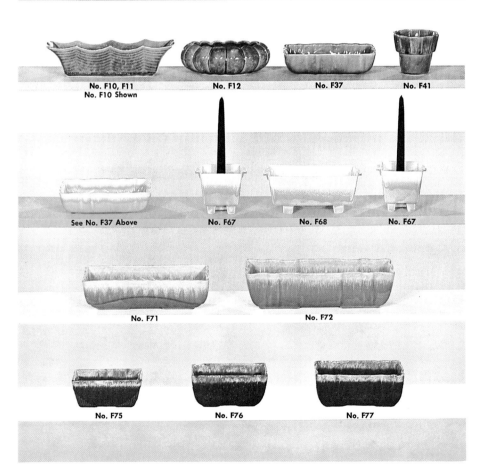

| No. F3 | No. F7 | No. F8 | No. F9 |

No. F10, F11
No. F10 Shown

| No. F12 | No. F37 | No. F41 |

| See No. F37 Above | No. F67 | No. F68 | No. F67 |

| No. F71 | No. F72 |

| No. F75 | No. F76 | No. F77 |

Imperial Ware By HULL

Novelty Planter
Jardinieres Vases

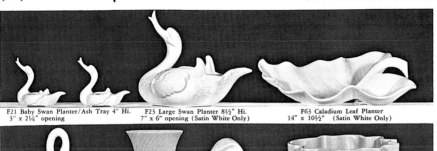

F21 Baby Swan Planter/Ash Tray 4" Hi.
3" x 2¼" opening

F23 Large Swan Planter 8½" Hi.
7" x 6" opening (Satin White Only)

F63 Caladium Leaf Planter
14" x 10½"   (Satin White Only)

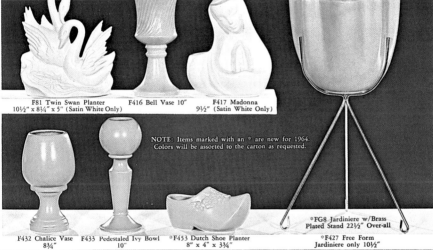

F81 Twin Swan Planter
10½" x 8¼" x 5" (Satin White Only)

F416 Bell Vase 10"

F417 Madonna
9½" (Satin White Only)

NOTE: Items marked with an * are new for 1964.
Colors will be assorted to the carton as requested.

*FG8 Jardiniere w/Brass
Plated Stand 22½" Over-all

F432 Chalice Vase
8¾"

F433 Pedestaled Ivy Bowl
10"

*F453 Dutch Shoe Planter
8" x 4" x 3¾"

*F427 Free Form
Jardiniere only 10½"

*F459 Cylindrical Vase
4⅜" dia. x 10¾"

*F460 Embossed Chalice Vase
5⅜" dia. x 9"

*F461 Pitcher Vase
11¾" Hi.

*F462 Pedestaled Rose Vase
5" dia. x 10⅞"

Hull Pottery Company - - Crooksville, Ohio

Vases

Imperial

SW—Satin White
MG—Moss Green
SG—Spring Green
CP—Carnation Pink
L—Lilac

Planters

F410
Pedestaled Flower Bowl
6" Dia. x 4¾"

F411
Square Footed Planter
5½" x 4¾" Hi.

F412
Urn Planter
5¼" Dia. x 5"

F413
Twisted Square Vase
8½"

F414
Small Neck Vase
10"

F415
Shell Vase
9"

F416
Bell Vase
10"

—— *Special Imperial Urn Vases* ——

Satin White and Moss Green Only.   **Note: Packed in special containers for your convenience.**

F418
Urn Vase
5" Hi.—3" opening

F419
Urn Vase
6" Hi.—4" opening

F420
Urn Vase
7" Hi.—5" opening

F421
Urn Vase
8" Hi.—6" opening

 Hull Pottery Company - - Crooksville, Ohio

Dish Gardens

Imperial

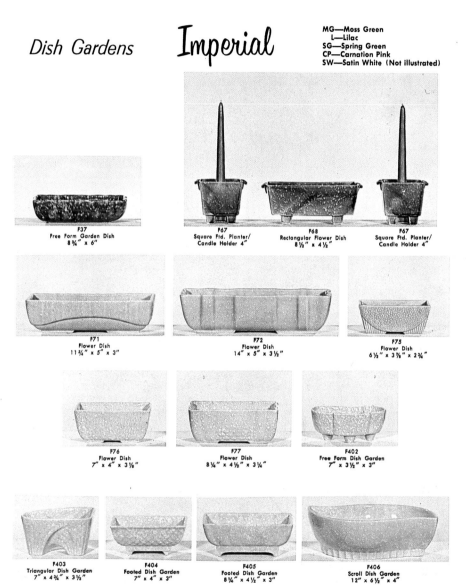

F37
Free Form Garden Dish
8¾" x 6"

F67
Square Ftd. Planter/
Candle Holder 4"

F68
Rectangular Flower Dish
8½" x 4½"

F67
Square Ftd. Planter/
Candle Holder 4"

F71
Flower Dish
11¾" x 5" x 3"

F72
Flower Dish
14" x 5" x 3½"

F75
Flower Dish
6½" x 3⅞" x 2¾"

F76
Flower Dish
7" x 4" x 3⅛"

F77
Flower Dish
8¼" x 4½" x 3¼"

F402
Free Form Dish Garden
7" x 3½" x 3"

F403
Triangular Dish Garden
7" x 4¾" x 3½"

F404
Footed Dish Garden
7" x 4" x 3"

F405
Footed Dish Garden
8¼" x 4½" x 3"

F406
Scroll Dish Garden
12" x 6½" x 4"

Hull Pottery Company - - Crooksville, Ohio

205

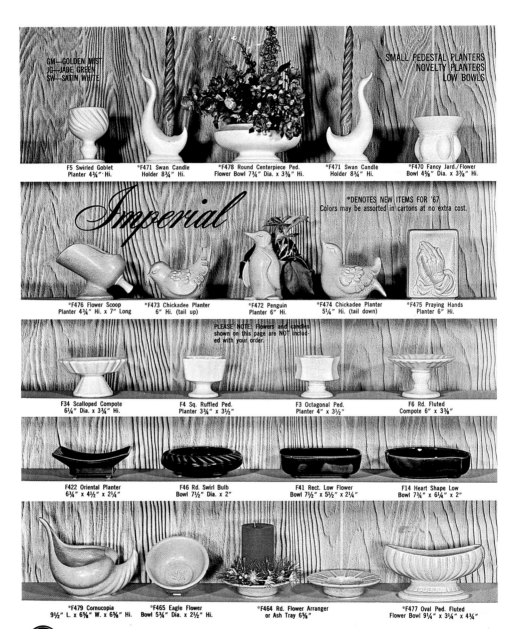

GM—GOLDEN MIST
JG—JADE GREEN
SW—SATIN WHITE

SMALL PEDESTAL PLANTERS
NOVELTY PLANTERS
LOW BOWLS

F5 Swirled Goblet
Planter 4¾" Hi.

°F471 Swan Candle
Holder 8¾" Hi.

°F478 Round Centerpiece Ped.
Flower Bowl 7¾" Dia. x 3⅜" Hi.

°F471 Swan Candle
Holder 8¾" Hi.

°F470 Fancy Jard./Flower
Bowl 4⅝" Dia. x 3⅞" Hi.

Imperial

°DENOTES NEW ITEMS FOR '67
Colors may be assorted in cartons at no extra cost.

°F476 Flower Scoop
Planter 4¾" Hi. x 7" Long

°F473 Chickadee Planter
6" Hi. (tail up)

°F472 Penguin
Planter 6" Hi.

°F474 Chickadee Planter
5¼" Hi. (tail down)

°F475 Praying Hands
Planter 6" Hi.

PLEASE NOTE: Flowers and candles
shown on this page are NOT included with your order.

F34 Scalloped Compote
6¼" Dia. x 3¾" Hi.

F4 Sq. Ruffled Ped.
Planter 3¾" x 3½"

F3 Octagonal Ped.
Planter 4" x 3½"

F6 Rd. Fluted
Compote 6" x 3⅜"

F422 Oriental Planter
6¾" x 4½" x 2¼"

F46 Rd. Swirl Bulb
Bowl 7½" Dia. x 2"

F41 Rect. Low Flower
Bowl 7½" x 5½" x 2¼"

F14 Heart Shape Low
Bowl 7¾" x 6¼" x 2"

°F479 Cornucopia
9½" L. x 6⅝" W. x 6⅝" Hi.

°F465 Eagle Flower
Bowl 5¾" Dia. x 2½" Hi.

°F464 Rd. Flower Arranger
or Ash Tray 6⅝"

°F477 Oval Ped. Fluted
Flower Bowl 9¼" x 3¼" x 4¾"

hull pottery company — crooksville, ohio *u.s.a.*

206

GM—GOLDEN MIST
JG—JADE GREEN
SW—SATIN WHITE

Imperial

VASES
LARGE PEDESTAL PLANTERS
SWANS
MADONNA

F50 Rose Vase
9½" Hi. x 4½" Dia.

F417 Madonna (large)
9½" (Satin White only)

F51 Rose Vase
12" Hi. x 5½" Dia.

°DENOTES NEW ITEMS FOR '67
Colors may be assorted in cartons at no extra cost.

F33 Fancy Oval
Vase 5½" Hi.

F21 Baby Swan Planter/Ash Tray
4" Hi.—3" x 2¼" opening
(Satin White only)

F23 Large Swan Planter
8½" Hi.—7" x 6" opening
(Satin White only)

F21 Baby Swan Planter/Ash Tray
4" Hi.—3" x 2¼" opening
(Satin White only)

F35 Urn Planter
5¾" Dia. x 5½" Hi.

F425 Footed Octagonal
Compote 7½" x 4¼"

815 Swan Ash Tray
or Planter 4½" x 4"

812 Swan Planter or
Centerpiece 9" x 7½"

815 Swan Ash Tray
or Planter 4½" x 4"

F44 Large off-square Pedestal
Planter 5½" x 5½" x 5"

°F481 Eagle Vase
10" Hi.

°F480 Swirl Pitcher
Vase 10¾" Hi.

°F482 Gurgling Fish
Pitcher Vase 11" Hi.

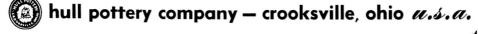

hull pottery company — crooksville, ohio *u.s.a.*

207

FLOWER CLUB CERAMICS

IN SATIN WHITE · JADE GREEN · WILD HONEY

890
Individual
Leaf Dish
7¼" x 5"

891
3 Compartment
Leaf Shape
Chip n' Dip
12¼" x 9"

821
Grecian Urn
5" x 5½"

822
Flower Basket
7"

823
Pedestaled Planter
4¾" x 5¾"

*Hull Pottery Company,
Crooksville, Ohio*

824
Leaf Shaped Flower Bowl
9¾" x 7" x 2½"

825
Low Bowl with Scallops
9¾" x 6" x 2"

826
Square Pagoda Plan
6" sq.

827
Pagoda Flower Bowl
7½" x 5¼" x 4"

828
Usubata Jardiniere
7¼" x 4½"

829
Dish Garden
6" x 3½" x 2⅛"

830
Dish Garden
6½" x 3¾" x 2¾"

831
Compote
6½" dia. x 7" hi.

MILK WHITE W/GREEN TRIM (only)

SATIN WHITE (only)

815
Baby Swan Planter
4½" x 4"

812
Swan Planter
9" x 7½"

213
Swan Centerpiece
or Planter
7½" x 9½" x 10"

813
Madonna Planter
9" x 7½"
Printed in U.S.A.

208

HULL POTTERY COMPANY, Crooksville, Ohio

201 — 5" x 3½"
also
201 — 5½" x 4"

202 — 6¾" x 3¼" x 4"

203 — 5¼"

204 — 5¼"

206 — 6¾" x 3¾" x 3"

207 — 8" x 3" x 3¾"

208 — 8½" x 4¼" x 3¼"

205B
14½" Overall High

209 — 9"

210 — 9"

211 — 10½"

212

213

NO. 125

NO. 63

NO. 126

HULL POTTERY CO., CROOKSVILLE, OHIO

210

NO.53 NO.54 NO.67

NO.56 NO.57 NO.64

NO.62

HULL POTTERY CO., CROOKSVILLE OHIO

211

"Cook 'N' Serve Ware"

**ALL ITEMS ILLUSTRATED MAY BE HAD IN EITHER
GREEN/BROWN FLOW GLAZE OR BLACK/WHITE**

#17C IND. COV. HDLD. CASSEROLE
$7.20 DOZ.　　PKD. 2 DOZ.
WT. 31 LBS. PKD.

#12 1½ QT. CASSEROLE & COVER
$12.00 DZ.　　PKD. 1 DOZ.
WT. 48 LBS. PKD.

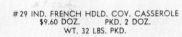

#29 IND. FRENCH HDLD. COV. CASSEROLE
$9.60 DOZ.　　PKD. 2 DOZ.
WT. 32 LBS. PKD.

#26 16-OZ. HANDLED MUG
$7.20 DOZ.　PKD. 2 DOZ.
WT. 32 LBS. PKD.

#28 1½ QT. FRENCH HDLD. COV. CASSEROLE
$18.00 DOZ.　　PKD. ½ DOZ.
WT. 24 LBS. PKD.

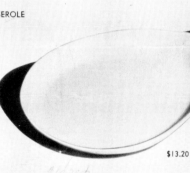

#27 LGE.
HDLD. SKILLET
15½" OVERALL

#30 SMALL HDLD. SKILLET 10" OVERALL
$6.60 DOZ.　　PKD. 2 DOZ.
WT. 16 LBS.

$13.20 DOZ.　　PKD. 2 DOZ.
WT. 43 LBS.

ALL PRICES WHOLESALE

F.O.B. CROOKSVILLE, OHIO

TERMS: 2/10 NET 30.

A. H. Dorman

212

"Cook 'N' Serve Ware"

ALL ITEMS ILLUSTRATED MAY BE HAD IN *EITHER*
GREEN/BROWN FLOW GLAZE OR *BLACK/WHITE*

#23 TEAPOT & COVER
$18.00 DOZ.
PKD. ½ DOZ.
WT. 20 LBS. PKD.

#24-25 COV. SUGAR & CREAMER
$16.50 DOZ. SETS.   PKD. ½ DOZ. SETS
WT. 15 LBS. PKD.

#20 CEREAL BOWL
$3.75 DOZ.   PKD. 2 DOZ.
WT. 17 LBS. PKD.

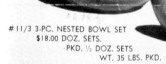

#11/3 3-PC. NESTED BOWL SET
$18.00 DOZ. SETS.
PKD. ½ DOZ. SETS
WT. 35 LBS. PKD.

#18 COV. SNACK JAR
$16.50 DOZ.   PKD. ½ DOZ.
WT. 23 LBS. PKD.

#22 2-QT. ICE JUG
$18.00 DZ.   PKD. ½ DZ.
WT. 20 LBS.

#14-15 S/P
$13.20 DZ. PRS.
PKD. 1 DZ. PRS.
WT. 25 LBS.

#16 1-QT. JUG
$10.50 DZ.   PKD. 1 DZ.
WT. 22 LBS.

213

No. 81
Madonna Planter
8" x 7"

No. 83
Novelty Hand
with Cornucopia Vase
7 ¾"

No. 84
Mandolin Planter
or Wall Pocket
7 ¼"

No. 85
Bass Viol Planter
or Wall Pocket
7 ¼"

No. 86
Deep Leaf Flower Bowl
9 ½" x 7" x 3 ½"

No. 82
Circus Clown Planter
6 ½" x 8 ½"

No. 95
Chinese Rooster Planter
or Center Piece
10" x 7 ½" x 8 ¼"

No. 87
Footed Oval Flower Bowl
10" x 4 ¾" x 4"

HULL POTTE

No. 88
Candle Lite Flower Bowl
11" x 4½" x 4"
(Candle NOT included)

No. 91
Consolette (Flower Bowl
with Built-in Candle Holders)
(Candles NOT included)
13½" x 4¾" x 5"

No. 92B
Brass Table Stand with
7" No. 92 High-Flower and Leaf Etched
Jardiniere
7½" High Overall

No. 93B
Brass Floor Stand with
8½" x 8½" No. 93 Jardiniere
16" High Overall

No. 94B
High-Bucket Jardiniere
with Metal Bail
9" x 9"

RY COMPANY, Crooksville, Ohio

215

No. 86
Deep Leaf Flower Bowl
9½" x 7" x 3½"

No. 88
Candle Lite Flower Bowl
11" x 4½" x 4"
(Candle NOT included)

No. 81
Madonna Planter
8" x 7"

No. 87
Footed Oval Flower Bowl
10" x 4¾" x 4"

No. 93B
Brass Floor Stand with
8½" x 8½" No. 93 Jardiniere
16" High Overall

No. 92B
Brass Table Stand with
7" No. 92 High-Flower and Leaf Etched
Jardiniere
7½" High Overall

No. 94B
High-Bucket Jardiniere
with Metal Bail
9" x 9"

HULL POTTERY COMPANY   Crooksville, Ohio

FLOWERWARE

No. 71
Flower Arranger Vase
9"

Cost $6.60 Dz. — Sell $1.00 Ea.
Pk. ½ Dz. Ctn., Wt. 16 lbs.

No. 74
Window Box with Scalloped Top
13"x4¼"x3"

Cost $6.60 Dz. — Sell $1.00 Ea.
Pk. 2/3 Dz. Ctn., Wt. 18 lbs.

No. K-200
Combination Ash Tray and Planter Bowl
26½" High

Cost $1.75 Ea. — Sell $2.98 Ea.
Pk. 12 only sets, Wt. 78 lbs.

No. 79C
Footed Candy Dish and Cover with Brass Knob
8¼"x6½"

Cost $12.60 Dz. — Sell $1.95 Ea.
Pk. ½ Dz. Ctn., Wt. 18 lbs.

No. 79
Footed Round Planter Bowl
6½"x5½"

Cost $8.16 Dz. — Sell $1.29 Ea.
Pk. ½ Dz. Ctn., Wt. 11 lbs.

K 30 W
Classic 6" Jardiniere
with Brass Stand
7½" High
Cost $ .81 Ea.
Sell $1.49 Ea.
Pk. 12 only sets, Wt. 28 lbs.

M 30 W
Classic 8" Jardiniere
with Brass Stand
15" High
(see listing)

O 75 W
Lantern 7" Jardiniere
with Brass Stand
19" High
Cost $1.59 Ea. — Sell $1.98 Ea.
Pk. 6 only sets, Wt. 33 lbs.

G 8
Contemporary 10" Jardiniere
with Brass Stand
21" High
(see listing)

HULL POTTERY COMPANY : : **Crooksville, Ohio**

Fantastic FANTASY $1 Retail Assortment

No. 71
Flower Arranger Vase
9"

No. 37
Chinese Vase
8"

65
Urn-Vase
5¾"

No. 74
Window Box with Scalloped Top
13"x4¼"x3"

No. 35
Modern Garden Dish
8½"x5"x3"

No. 36
Victorian Flower Bowl
9¼"x3¾"x4"

No. 38
Pedestaled Square Planter
4¾"x5½"

Nos. 71, 37, 38, 74, 35 and 36 are made in three decorations: [Dec. #1 — Pink with Turquoise Foam.
No. 65 is made in two colors: Milk White, Black with White Foam. [Dec. #2 — Turquoise with White Foam.
[Dec. #3 — Black with White Foam.

Colors may be assorted as wanted to the assortment.

HULL POTTERY COMPANY, Crooksville, Ohio

65—5¾" Urn-Vase

W16—8½" Vase

W10—11" Cornucopia

W18—11" Vase

E7—11" Vase

80—Swan Planter (6" x 6" x 7½")
69—Swan Planter (8½" x 8½" x 10½")
70—Swan Ash Tray (4½" x 4½")

#27—11½"
Standing Madonna
with Planter Urns

89—11½" St. Francis Planter

Hull Pottery Company - - **Crooksville, Ohio**

No. 101—8

No. 102—11"

No. 112—10"

No. 210—9"

No. 211—10½"

No. 203—5½" x 4½"

No. 206—6¾ x3¾ x3

No. 208—8½ x4¼ x3½"

M 30 W
Classic 8 Jardiniere
with Brass Stand
15" High

G 8
Contemporary 10" Jardiniere
with Brass Stand
21" High

HULL POTTERY COMPANY, Crooksville, Ohio

220

65
Urn-Vase
5¾"

No. 74
Window Box with Scalloped Top
13"x4¼"x3"

No. K-200
Combination Ash Tray and Planter Bowl
26½" High

No. 94B
High-Bucket Jardiniere
with Metal Bail
9" x 9"

No. 93W
Wrought Iron Floor Stand with
8½" x 8½" No. 93 Jardiniere
16" High Overall

K 30 W
Classic 6" Jardiniere
with Brass Stand
7½" High

M 30 W
Classic 8" Jardiniere
with Brass Stand
15" High

M30
As above except
with Wrought Iron Stand

G 8
Contemporary 10" Jardiniere
with Brass Stand
21" High

HULL POTTERY COMPANY, Crooksville, Ohio

K 200

ASH TRAY AND PLANTER WITH METAL STAND

available in:

Decoration C Charcoal with White veiling
Decoration D Willow Green with Black veiling
Decoration A Pink with Black veiling

Minimum quantity available is one dozen complete sets
16½ lbs. per set) in the three color combinations which
may be assorted at no extra cost.

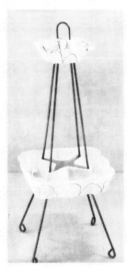

K100—Ash Tray and Planter
with Metal Stand

K300 — Heart Shaped Ash Tray
with Metal Stand 26½" high.

M30—Classic Jardiniere (8");
Metal Stand (15" high)

80—Swan Planter (6" x 6" x 7½")
69—Swan Planter (8½" x 8½" x 10½")
70—Swan Ash Tray (4½" x 4½")

N75—2 Lantern Jardinieres (6");
Metal Stand (16" high)

75—6" Jardiniere
75—7" Jardiniere

#24—7¼"
Praying Madonna
Planter Vase

#25—7¼"
Kneeling Madonna
Planter Vase

#26—7"
Madonna with
Child Planter Vase

#27—11½"
Standing Madonna
with Planter Urns

89—11½" St. Francis Planter

HULL POTTERY COMPANY   **CROOKSVILLE, OHIO**

Printed in U. S. A.

223

Satin Finish Sun Valley Pastels

With NEW METAL ACCESSORIES

R 1 — Table Model
Jardiniere with Lantern—Metal Stand
10½" Overall

R 2 — Table Model
Jardiniere with Harp—Metal Stand
9" High x 6½" Wide Overall

R 3 — Floor Model
Jardiniere with Harp—Metal Stand
12" High x 11" Wide Overall

R 4 — Table Model
Flower Dish with Gondola—Metal Stand
16" Long x 5½" Wide Overall

R 5 — Floor Model
3 Jardinieres with Step Down—Metal Stand
18" Long x 17" High Overall

R 7 — Floor Model
3 Jardinieres with Tree—Metal Stand
30" High Overall

HULL POTTERY CO.   **Crooksville, Ohio**

816—Printed in U. S. A.

New Satin Finish *Sun Valley Pastels*

WITH

NEW WROUGHT IRON ACCESSORIES

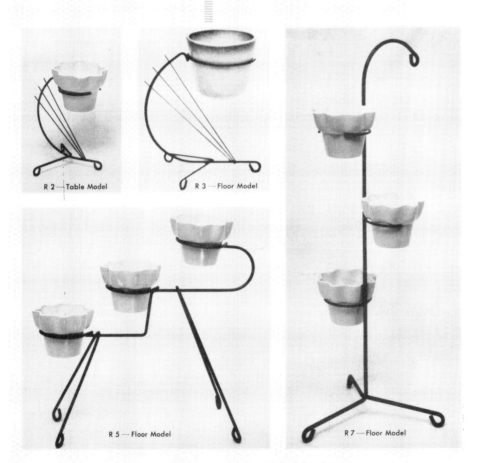

R 2 — Table Model

R 3 — Floor Model

R 5 — Floor Model

R 7 — Floor Model

See list for color choice, price, weight and package

HULL POTTERY COMPANY : : : : Crooksville, Ohio

For Your Special Sales Days

Why Not Try . .

K 200
ASH TRAY AND PLANTER WITH METAL STAND
Beautiful New Decorations

Decoration: 1. Pink with Turquoise Foam
Decoration: 2. Turquoise with White Foam
Decoration: 3. Black with White Foam

(Decorations may be assorted to the carton)

Minimum Quantity: 12 Only Sets to Cartons.
Weight 78 Pounds

It's a Proven Traffic Builder

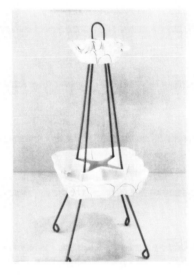

K100—Ash Tray and Planter
with Metal Stand

K200—Heart Shaped Ash Tray and
Planter with Metal Stand 26½" high

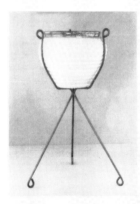

M30—Classic Jardiniere (8");
Metal Stand (15" high)

075—Lantern Jardiniere (7");
Metal Stand (19" high)

N75—2 Lantern Jardinieres (6");
Metal Stand (16" high)

Hull Pottery Company - - **Crooksville, Ohio**

Red Hot . . .

Year Around Sellers!

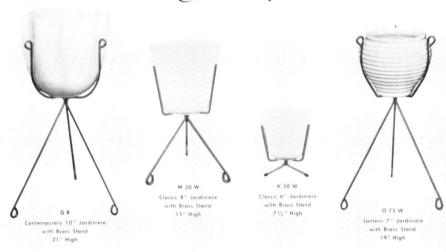

G 8
Contemporary 10" Jardiniere
with Brass Stand
21" High

M 30 W
Classic 8" Jardiniere
with Brass Stand
15" High

K 30 W
Classic 6" Jardiniere
with Brass Stand
7½" High

O 75 W
Lantern 7" Jardiniere
with Brass Stand
19" High

(See your listing for prices and packages).

- Sell them for use on porch or patio!

- Sell them for use as cemetery urns!

- Sell them for use in living room!

- Sell them for use as ice bucket!

- Sell them for use wherever smart containers for plants or flowers are desired!

High Fashion . . .

HULL POTTERY COMPANY : : Crooksville, Ohio

228

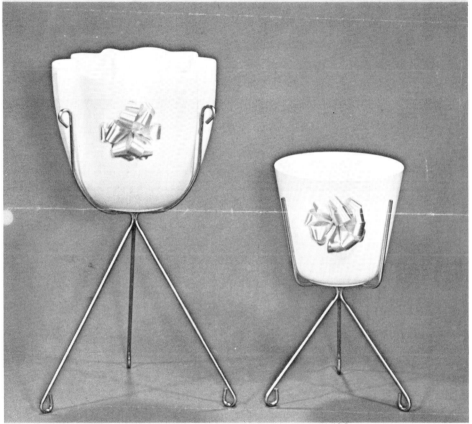

229

Available in Satin White and Moss Green only.

No. F4

No. F5

No. F14

No. F15

No. F19, F19B, F20, F20B

No. F27

No. F28, F29
No. F29 Shown

No. F31, F32, F33
No. F33 Shown

No. F34, F35, F36
No. F35 Shown

No. F38

No. F39

No. F43

No. F44

No. F45

No. F46

No. F47

No. F48

No. F49, F50
No. F50 Shown

No. F57

Hull Pottery Company - - Crooksville, Ohio

Page 3—See page 3 in Price List
Available in Satin White and
Moss Green only.

No. F63

No. F64

No. F73

Spiral

No. F82

Available in Satin White, Moss Green
and Mahogany with White Flow

No. F83

No. F84

No. F85

No. F86

Unusual
PLANTERS

Available in Satin White only

No. F21, F22, F23
No. F23 Shown

No. F40

No. F80

No. F81

No. F89

231

NOVELTY PLANTERS
JARDINIERES

Imperial Ware

SW—Satin White
JG—Jade Green
WH—Wild Honey

F21—Baby Swan Planter/Ash Tray
4" Hi x 3" x 2¼" opening
F23—Large Swan Planter
8½" Hi—7" x 6" opening
(Satin White only Shown Above)

F41
Flower Pot
3¾" x 4½"

F43
Urn Jardiniere
5¾" x 5½"

F63
Caladium Leaf Planter
14" L. x 10½" W.

F81—Twin Swan Planter
10½" x 8¼" x 5"
(Satin White only)

F417—Madonna
9½"
(Satin White only)

F420—Urn Vase
7" Hi.—5" opening
F419—Urn Vase
6" Hi.—4" opening
(Not Shown)
F418—Urn Vase
5" Hi.—3" opening
(Not Shown)

F426—Square
Oriental Jardiniere
5" x 4"

F428
Usubata Planter
5¼" x 3¾"

F431—Square Oriental Bowl
w/Round Opening
5½" x 6½" x 4" opening

F443
Panelled Jardiniere
9" x 7"
(Not Shown)

F444
Panelled Jardiniere
10½" x 9½"

F429
Usubata Planter
7½" x 4½"

Hull Pottery Company - - Crooksville, Ohio

232

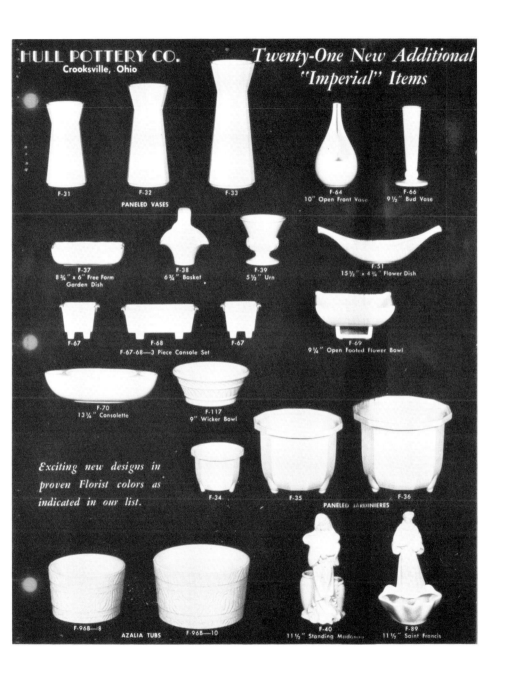

HULL POTTERY CO.
Crooksville, Ohio

Twenty-One New Additional
"Imperial" Items

F-31

F-32

F-33

PANELED VASES

F-64
10" Open Front Vase

F-66
9½" Bud Vase

F-37
8¾" x 6" Free Form
Garden Dish

F-38
6¾" Basket

F-39
5½" Urn

F-51
15½" x 4¾" Flower Dish

F-67

F-68

F-67

F-67-68—3 Piece Console Set

F-69
9¼" Open Footed Flower Bowl

F-70
13¼" Consolette

F-117
9" Wicker Bowl

Exciting new designs in
proven Florist colors as
indicated in our list.

F-34

F-35

F-36

PANELED JARDINIERES

F-96B—8

AZALIA TUBS

F-96B—10

F-40
11½" Standing Madonna

F-89
11½" Saint Francis

233

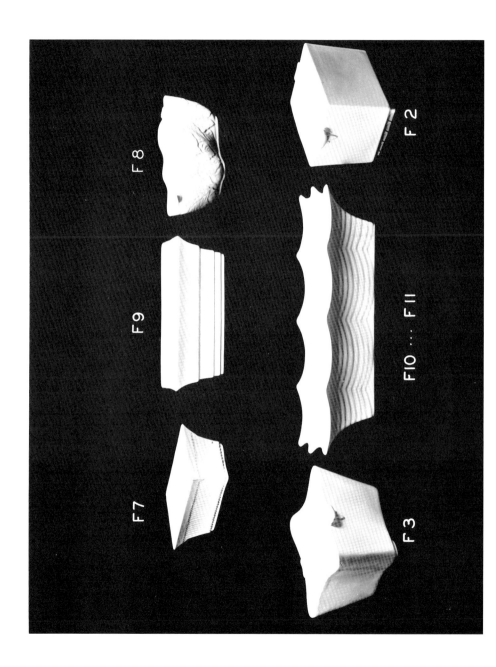

F 17

F 60

F18···F19···F20

F19B···F20B

F 1

F28···F29

F 71

235

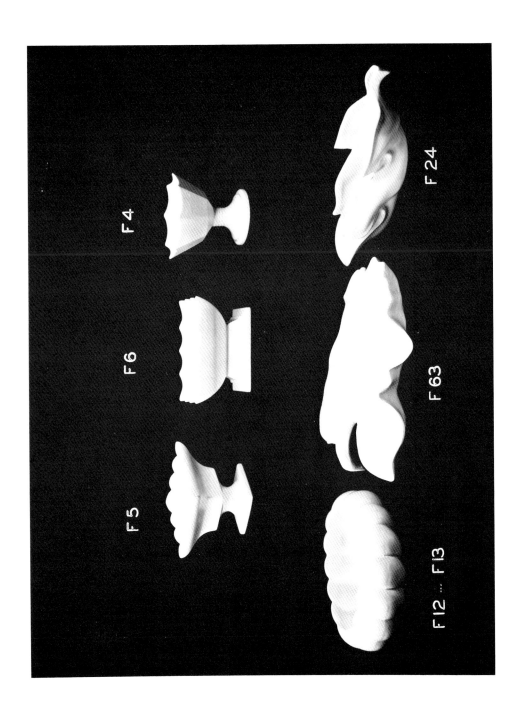

F 4

F 6

F 5

F 24

F 63

F 12 ··· F 13

236

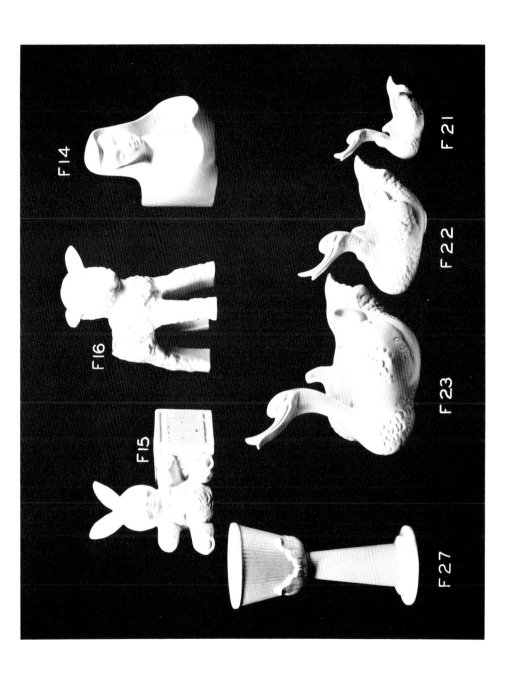

K 30 W
Classic 6" Jardiniere
with Brass Stand
7½" High

O 75 W
Lantern 7" Jardiniere
with Brass Stand
19" High

#K30W   6" JARDINIERE WITH BRASS STAND SET
EA.   .81   1.49   45%

.#075W   7" JARDINIERE WITH BRASS STAND SET
EA.   1.59   2.98   46%

G 8
Contemporary 10" Jardiniere
with Brass Stand
21" High

M40

Classic 8" Jardiniere
with Brass Stand
15" High

#G8   10" JARDINIERE WITH BRASS STAND SET
EA.   2.20   3.98   44%

#M40   8" JARDINIERE BRASS STAND SET
EA.   1.08   1.98   45%

Jardinieres Imperial

Planters

F19
Utility Jardiniere
9" Dia. x 7" Hi.

F20
Utility Jardiniere
10½" Dia. x 9½" Hi.
Shown

F34
Paneled Jardiniere

F39—Urn 5½

F41
Flower Pot
3¾" x 4½"

F43
Urn Jardiniere
5¾" x 5½"

F63
Caladium Leaf Planter
14" L. x 10½" W.

F64
Open Front Vase
10"

F401
Low Round Flower Bowl
6" Dia. x 3"

F407
Triangular Hanging Basket
8" x 5¼"

Religious and Novelty Planters in Satin White Only.

F21—Baby Swan Planter/Ash Tray
4" H. x 3" x 2¼" opening

F22—Medium Swan Planter
6" Hi. x 7¼" L—4¼" x 4" opening

F23—Large Swan Planter
8½" H.—7" x 6" opening (Shown)

F81
Twin Swan Planter
10½" x 8¼" x 5"

F408
Cherub Girl Planter
5¾"

F409
Cherub Boy Planter
5¾"

F417
Madonna
9½

Hull Pottery Company - - Crooksville, Ohio

239

Vases — Planters
Flower Bowls

Imperial Ware

SW—Satin White
JG—Jade Green
WH—Wild Honey

F401
Low Round Flower Bowl
6" Dia. x 3"

F410
Pedestaled Flower Bowl
6" Dia. x 4¾"

F411
Square Footed Planter
5½" x 4¾" Hi.

F412
Urn Planter
5¼" Dia. x 5"

F416
Bell Vase
10"

F422
Oriental Planter
6¾" x 4½" x 2¼"

F425
Octagonal Compote
7½" x 4¼"

F430
Footed Round Flower Bowl
5¾" Dia. x 4" Hi. x 3½"
opening

F432
Chalice Vase
8¾"

F433
Pedestaled Ivy Vase
10"

F434
Urn Vase
7"

F435
Bud Vase
9"

F445
Candle Holder
4½" Hi.

F436
Float Bowl Console
11" x 8" x 1¾"

F445
Candle Holder
4½" Hi.

F439
Usubata Vase
8½"

 Hull Pottery Company - - Crooksville, Ohio

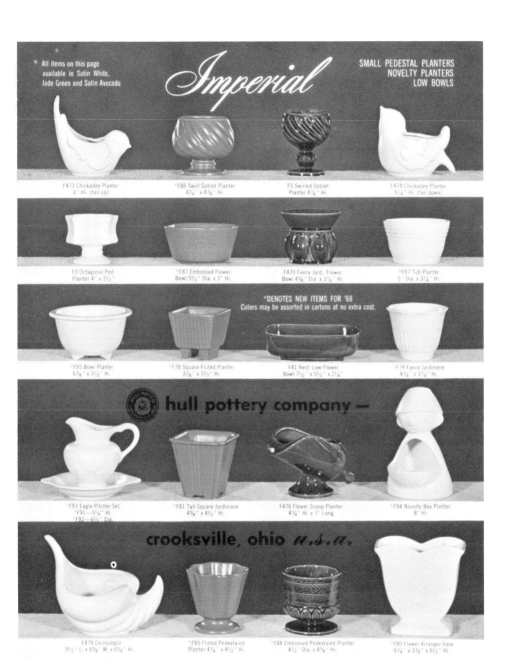

All items on this page available in Satin White, Jade Green and Satin Avocado

Imperial

SMALL PEDESTAL PLANTERS
NOVELTY PLANTERS
LOW BOWLS

F473 Chickadee Planter
6" Hi. (tail up)

*F86 Swirl Goblet Planter
4⅞" x 4⅜" Hi.

F5 Swirled Goblet
Planter 4¼" Hi.

F474 Chickadee Planter
5¼" Hi. (tail down)

F3 Octagonal Ped.
Planter 4" x 3½"

*F87 Embossed Flower
Bowl 5½" Dia. x 3" Hi.

F470 Fancy Jard. Flower
Bowl 4⅝" Dia. x 3½" Hi.

*F97 Tub Planter
5" Dia. x 3¼" Hi.

*DENOTES NEW ITEMS FOR '68
Colors may be assorted in cartons at no extra cost.

*F95 Bowl Planter
6⅜" x 3½" Hi.

*F78 Square Fluted Planter
3⅞" x 3½" Hi.

F41 Rect. Low Flower
Bowl 7½" x 5½" x 2¼"

*F79 Fancy Jardiniere
4¾" x 3⅜" Hi.

hull pottery company —

*F93 Eagle Pitcher Set
*F91—5¼" Hi.
*F92—6½" Dia.

*F81 Tall Square Jardiniere
4⅝" x 4½" Hi.

F476 Flower Scoop Planter
4¾" Hi. x 7" Long

*F94 Novelty Boy Planter
8" Hi.

crooksville, ohio *u.s.a.*

F479 Cornucopia
9½" L x 6⅜" W x 6⅝" Hi.

*F85 Fluted Pedestaled
Planter 4¾" x 4½" Hi.

*F84 Embossed Pedestaled Planter
4½" Dia. x 4⅜" Hi.

*F90 Flower Arranger Vase
6¾" x 3⅜" x 6½" Hi.

241

Dish Garden　　　　*Imperial Ware*

F71
Dish Garden
11¾" x 5" x 3"

F72
Dish Garden
14" x 5" x 3½"

F75
Dish Garden
6½" x 3⅝" x 2¾"

F76
Dish Garden
7" x 4" x 3⅛"

F77
Dish Garden
8¼" x 4½" x 3½"

F402
Free Fair Dish Garden
7" x 3½" x 3"

F403
Triangular Dish Garden
7" x 4¾" x 3½"

F404
Footed Dish Garden
7" x 4" x 3

F405
Footed Dish Garden
8¼" x 4½" x 3"

F406
Scroll Dish Garden
12" x 6½" x 4"

F423
Low Flower Bowl
8¼" x 6" x 2"

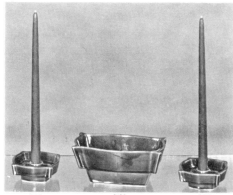

F424
Low Flower Bowl or Ash Tray
10¼" x 6¼" x 1½"

F437
Candle Holder
4½" x 4½" x 1¾

F438
Console Flower Bowl
8¾" x 4¾" x 3½"

F437
Candle Holder
4½" x 4½" x 1¾

Hull Pottery Company -- Crooksville, Ohio

Designed Especially for Florists
by Hull

F65 Lg. Ruffled Top Ped. Planter
7¾" x 5¼"

F25 Rnd. Ped. Planter
7½" Dia. x 4⅛" Hi.

F425 Ftd. Oct. Compote
7½" x 4¼"

F88 Sculptured Ped.
Planter 5¼" x 5⅝"

F84 Emb. Ped.
Planter 4½" x 4⅜"

A54 Rnd. Ped. Planter
4" Dia. Top x 5" Hi.

F24 Flower Basket
7" x 6¼" x 6"

°A12 Rnd. Flower Bowl
9¼" Dia. x 3" Hi.

F27 Rnd. Emb. Ped. Planter
6½" Dia. x 4" Hi.

°A53 Cornucopia
8¼" x 5¾" x 4½" Hi.

°A56 Rnd. Ped. Planter
5" Dia. x 7" Hi.

F90 Single
Bud Vase
6½" Hi.

°A57 Rnd. Ped. Vase
4½" Dia. x 9¼" Hi

F61 Madonna (Large) 8½"
(Satin White Only)

F91 Eagle Pitcher Vase
5¼"
F92 Saucer For Eagle Pitcher Vase
6½" Dia.

°A50 Rose Emb. Pitcher
Vase 6¾"
°A51 Saucer For Pitcher
7" Dia.

F7 Basket
5¼" Dia. x 9" Hi.

(Satin White Only)

F815 Swan
Ashtray/Planter
4½" x 4"

(Satin White Only)

F812 Swan
Planter/Centerpiece
9" x 7½"

F30 Flower Vase
10"

F67 Lg. Swirl Ped. Planter
5⅞" x 8⅛"

F89 Square Vase
3¼" x 3¼" x 9⅛" Hi.

F31 Urn Type Vase
7⅛" Dia. Top x 8½" Hi.

F32 Fancy Pitcher Vase
10"

Imperial *made especially for Florists*

Thirty new and colorful American ceramic designs by HULL to accentuate your beautiful flowers, and priced at preinflation levels through the medium of modern methods of production.

This is our response to requests from many important suppliers. Months of exhaustive study and preparation have culminated in these pieces and colors to meet all your requirements. From ordinary low-cost vehicles for transporting plants, to beautiful containers for luxurious floral arrangements, you'll find everything you need and want in IMPERIAL.

Seven Beautiful Colors to Accent Your Arrangements:

• SATIN WHITE (SW)   • CARNATION PINK (CP)   • WILLOW GREEN (WG)
• SATIN BLACK (SB) • FROSTED BLACK (FB) • BITTERSWEET (BS) • MOSS GREEN (MG)

ABOVE LEFT: No. F4 — Octagonal Scalloped Pedestal Planter, 5" high with 5½" opening. Available in Satin White, Moss Green, Carnation Pink, Bittersweet, Willow Green and Frosted Black.

ABOVE CENTER: No. F63 — High-styled Caladium Leaf Planter, 14" long and 10½" wide. Available in Satin White, Moss Green and Bittersweet.

ABOVE RIGHT: No. F71 — Sleek Utility Vase with simple lines, 9½" high with 4½" opening. Available in Satin White, Moss Green, Carnation Pink, Bittersweet and Willow Green.

ABOVE LEFT: No. F5 — Square Scalloped Pedestal Planter, 4½" high with 5½" opening. Available in Satin White, Moss Green, Carnation Pink, Bittersweet, Willow Green and Satin Black.

ABOVE CENTER: No. F24 — Deep Leaf Planter. Measures a generous 12¼" x 5½" x 4½". Available in Satin White, Moss Green, Bittersweet and Frosted Black.

ABOVE RIGHT: No. F17 — Scalloped Pedestal Jardiniere, 6⅝" high with 6" diameter opening. Available in Satin White, Moss Green, Carnation Pink and Bittersweet.

ABOVE LEFT: No. F6 — Rectangular Scalloped Pedestal Planter, 4" high with 7" x 3" opening. Available in Satin White, Moss Green, Carnation Pink, Bittersweet, Willow Green and Frosted Black.

ABOVE CENTER: No. F3 — Pinched Planter with Lug Handles, 4½" high with 6" x 4" opening. Available in Satin White, Moss Green, Carnation Pink, Bittersweet, Willow Green and Satin Black.

ABOVE RIGHT: No. F27 — Stately Chalice Vase, 9" high with 3" opening. Available in Satin White and Carnation Pink.

ABOVE LEFT: No. F11 — Oval Fluted Bulb Bowl, 3½" high with 7½" x 4¾" opening. Available in Satin White, Moss Green, Carnation Pink and Bittersweet. (Smaller size of above) No. F12 — 3" high with 6½" x 4¼" opening. Same color choice.

ABOVE CENTER: No. F13 — Rectangular Garden Dish, 2" high with 6" x 4" opening. Available in Satin White, Moss Green, Carnation Pink, Bittersweet and Satin Black.

ABOVE RIGHT: No. F18 — Utility Jardiniere, 5½" high with 6" diameter opening. Available in Moss Green, Bittersweet and Gloss White.

ABOVE LEFT: No. F60 — Modern Display Vase, 15" high with 10" opening. Available in Satin White, Moss Green, Carnation Pink, Bittersweet and Willow Green.

ABOVE RIGHT: No. F39B — Utility Jardiniere with Brass Stand, 20" high overall. Jardiniere only, No. F39, 9½" high with 10½" opening. Smaller size available as No. F39B — Utility Jardiniere with Brass Stand, 15" high overall. Jardiniere only, No. F34, 7" high with 8" opening. These Jardinieres available in Moss Green, Bittersweet and Gloss White.

BELOW RIGHT: No. F29 — Rose Vase, 12" high with 5" opening. Smaller size available as No. F28 — Rose Vase, 9½" high with 4" opening. Both sizes in these colors: Moss Green, Carnation Pink, Bittersweet, Willow Green and Frosted Black.

BELOW LEFT: No. F31 — Rectangular Scalloped Garden Dish, 3½" high with 10½" x 5½" opening. Smaller size available as No. F30 — Rectangular Scalloped Garden Dish, 3" high with 12½" x 4¾" opening. Both of these Rectangular Scalloped Garden Dishes available in these colors: Satin White, Moss Green, Carnation Pink, Bittersweet and Willow Green.

ABOVE LEFT: No. F2 — Rectangular Pillow Vase, 4" high with 6" x 4" opening. Available in Satin White, Moss Green, Carnation Pink, Bittersweet, Willow Green and Frosted Black.

ABOVE CENTER: No. F5 — Rectangular Garden Dish, 3½" high with 8½" x 4½" opening. Available in Satin White, Moss Green, Carnation Pink, Bittersweet, Willow Green and Frosted Black.

ABOVE RIGHT: No. F1 — Crimped Top Jardiniere, 5½" high with 5"

Imperial by **Hull**

O W — Olive Trimmed in Willow Green
G T — Green Trimmed in Turquoise
S W — Satin White

Pedestaled Planters
Vases
Planters
Garden Dishes.

COLORS MAY BE A FOURTH IN CARTONS AT NO EXTRA COST

*DENOTES NEW ITEMS FOR 74

Victorian

*B31 Footed Pot
4" Dia. x 5" Hi

*B36 Footed Basket
7" Dia. x 9" Hi.

*B32 Footed Dish Garden
7" x 4" x 3½" Hi.

*B37 Vase
9" Hi.

ALL THE ABOVE ITEMS ARE NEW FOR 1974

FOLLOWING ARE BEST SELLING CARRY OVER ITEMS.

F7 Basket

F25 Rnd. Ped. Planter

F88 Sculptured Ped.

B12 Ped. Planter

F84 Emb. Ped.

F34 Urn Shaped Planter

A50 Rose Emb. Pitcher
A51 Saucer for Pitcher
7" Dia.

F91 Eagle Pitcher Vase
F92 Saucer For Eagle Pitcher Vase
6½" Dia.

F83 Pressed Ped. Planter
6" Dia. x 3½" Hi.

A54 Rnd. Ped. Planter
4" Dia. Top x 5" Hi.

F5 Swirl
Goblet Planter
4¾" Hi.

F3 Octagonal Ped. Planter
4" x 3½" Hi.

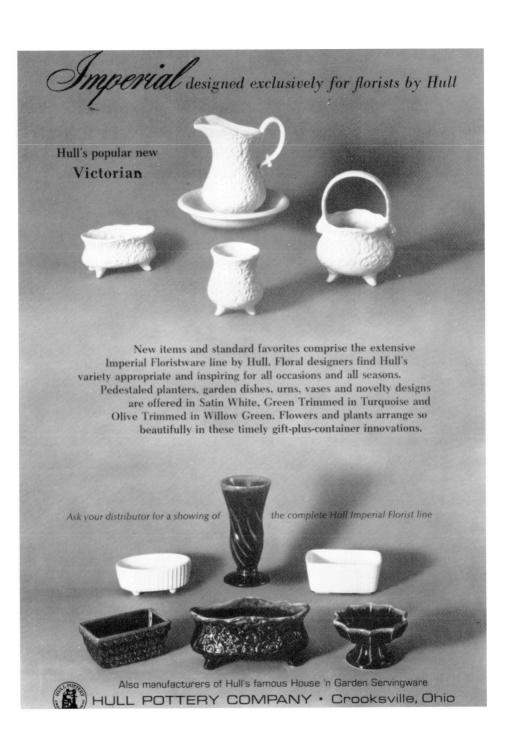

Imperial designed exclusively for florists by Hull

Hull's popular new
Victorian

New items and standard favorites comprise the extensive
Imperial Floristware line by Hull. Floral designers find Hull's
variety appropriate and inspiring for all occasions and all seasons.
Pedestaled planters, garden dishes, urns, vases and novelty designs
are offered in Satin White, Green Trimmed in Turquoise and
Olive Trimmed in Willow Green. Flowers and plants arrange so
beautifully in these timely gift-plus-container innovations.

Ask your distributor for a showing of   the complete Hull Imperial Florist line

Also manufacturers of Hull's famous House 'n Garden Servingware
HULL POTTERY COMPANY • Crooksville, Ohio

247

IMPERIAL
FLORISTWARE
BY HULL

DESIGNS
FOR FLORISTS WHO CREATE BEAUTIFUL THINGS WITH HULL'S IMPERIAL FLORISTWARE. OVER SIXTY ALL-OCCASION ITEMS ARE OFFERED IN SATIN WHITE, GREEN WITH TURQUOISE TRIM, AND OLIVE TRIMMED IN WILLOW GREEN. YOUR DISTRIBUTOR WILL GLADLY SHOW THEM ALL TO YOU.

Designed Exclusively for Florists

IMPERIAL FLORISTWARE by HULL

Floral designers find the variety in Hull's Imperial inspiring for all occasions and seasons. The sixty-plus line of garden dishes, urns, planters, vases, madonnas and novelty designs are offered in Satin White; Satin Avocado; Green trimmed in Turquoise; and Olive trimmed in Willow Green. Arrangements of flowers or plants in these moderately priced GIFT-plus-CONTAINER innovations are unlimited.

Designed Exclusively for Florists

Ask your distributor for a showing of the complete Hull Imperial Florist line

HULL POTTERY COMPANY • Crooksville, Ohio

GROWER COLLECTION

HULL POTTERY
327 AMERINE STREET
CROOKSVILLE, OHIO 43731

721
8¾" x 5½" x 4½"

719
6½" x 4¾" x 4"

720
8" x 5¾" x 4"

718
8¼" x 5½" x 4½"

717
7⅛" x 5½" x 4"

716
6⅛" x 4½" x 3½"

70
7" x 6½"

78
10½" x 5¼" x 3⅝"

71
9" x 5½" x 8"

69
10" x 5½" x 5¼"

HULL POTTERY   327 Amerine Street   Crooksville, Ohio 43731
614/982-2075   614/982-2085

1-83 5M CPC

250

*F66

* F66 Oval Handled Basket
7″ × 7″ High

* F67 Wicker Embossed Handled Basket
7½″ Long × 8″ High

Baskets are always best sellers!

Richly embossed floral and wicker patterns make them outstanding complements to every arrangement. Like the entire Imperial line, they are available in deep green, warm brown or satiny white to give them instant and long-lasting appeal.

† B36 Footed Basket
7″ Diameter × 9″ High

(Flowers and Macrame not included)

251

* F70 Caricature Frog
7" Wide × 6½" High

Hull's Aquatic Animals

Our aquatic animals will be pets in any setting. Their cheerful presence is perfect for rec-rooms, centerpieces or informal arrangements.

* F68 Caricature Hippo Planter
8½" Long × 5" Wide × 4¼" High

* F71 Swan
9" Long × 5½" Wide × 8" High

* F69 Duck Planter
10" Long × 5½" Wide × 5¼" High

HOUSE 'n GARDEN

STARTERSETS 'n PARTYPACKS

Hull's extensive open stock House 'n Garden Servingware is a standard favorite for today's casual way of living. The nations number one line offers over seventy five all-purpose pieces . . . . individual items, dinner sets, startersets and partypacks. Ovenproof House 'n Garden in the appealing Mirror Brown with Ivory Trim is timely, decorative and so useful for every indoor or outdoor serving occasion.

HULL POTTERY COMPANY • Crooksville, Ohio

OVENPROOF
Provincial
SERVING
WARE

700 Dinner Plate
10¼" Dia.

701 Salad Plate
6½" Dia.

703 Fruit
5¼"

702 Mug
9 oz.

722 Coffee Pot
w/cover (locking)
60 oz.

Four Piece Place Setting

705 Mixing Bowl
5¼"

706 Mixing Bowl
6¾"

707 Mixing Bowl
8½"

709 Water Jug
5 pint

725 Jug
2 pt.

718 Jug
½ pt.

710 Bean Pot
w/cover
2 qt.

724 Individual Bean
Pot w/cover
8 oz.

719 Sugar Bowl
w/cover
8 oz.

718 Creamer
8 oz.

711 Bake Dish
3 pt.

712 Casserole
w/cover
3 pt.

713 French Handled
Casserole
5¼"

727 French Handled
Casserole
w/cover

726 Beer Stein
16 oz.

714 Ice Jug
2 qt.

715 Salt Shaker
w/cork
3¾" Hi.

716 Pepper Shaker
w/cork
3¾" Hi.

721 Leaf Shaped
Chip 'n Dip
16" x 10½"

723 Cookie Jar
w/cover
94 oz.

Hull Pottery Company -- Crooksville, Ohio

255

Three New Sets

OVENPROOF $\mathcal{H}$ouse 'n $\mathcal{G}$arden *Serving-ware*

SOUP 'N SANDWICH

#555—8 pc. Set
Consisting of:
4 only #553 Soup Mugs 11 oz.
4 only #554 Trays

SNACK SET

#556—8 pc. Set
Consisting of:
4 only #502 Coffee Mugs 9 oz.
4 only #554 Trays

Beautiful tone of Mirror Brown trimmed in Ivory Foam. Packages are 200 lb. test reshipper. One set packed to a carton. Gross weight 8 lbs.

TOAST 'N CEREAL

57—8 pc. Set
sisting of:
nly #503 Cereal 12 oz.
nly #554 Trays

Hull Pottery Company, Crooksville, Ohio

256

beautiful new additions to the

OVENPROOF **H**ouse 'n

Garden Serving-ware

541
Individual Oval Steak Plate
11¾″ x 9″

542
Divided Vegetable
10¾″ x 7¼″

543
Open Oval Baker
10″ x 7¼″

544
Oval Casserole & Cover
10″ x 7¼″ (3 pt.)

545
Salad or Spaghetti Bowl
10¼″

547—Fork and
Spoon Set

S46—Three piece Salad Set consisting of:
1 only #545—Salad Bowl
1 only #547—Fork & Spoon Set

548
Oval Casserole & Cover
2 qt.—10″ x 7¼″

549
Tea Pot & Cover
5 cup

551
Jam or Mustard Jar & Cover
Set with Spoon
12 oz.

Hull Pottery Company, Crooksville, Ohio

257

HOUSE & GARDEN SERVING WARE

3-21-61

#80 - GIFTS, TABLEWARE ALL STORES NO. II4

258

CLASSIFICATION 1

Dept. 23
B.M.S. L-O
BDJV-1-2-3

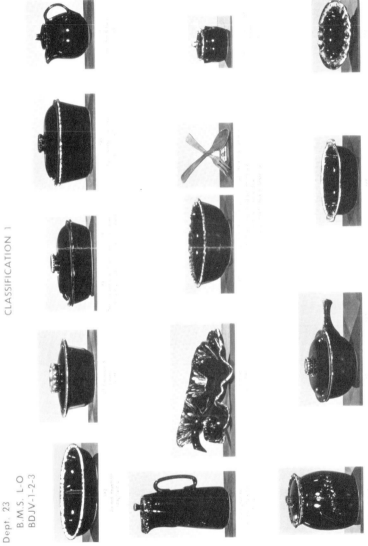

hull pottery company – crooksville, ohio *u.s.a.*

WATCH OUR "ADS" FOR THE BIG GALA
50th "Golden" Anniversary Dinnerware Coupons . . .

Made in U.S.A.

969
6½" Soup or Salad Bowl

900 Dinner Plate
10¼" Dia.
978—3 PIECE PLACE SETTING

902 Mug
9 oz.

970
Covered French Handled
Casserole w Warmer
3 pt.

926 Beer Stein
16 oz.

945—Salad or Spaghetti Bowl 10¼"   947—Fork and Spoon Set
946—Three piece Salad Set consisting of:
1 only #945—Salad Bowl
1 only #947—Fork & Spoon Set

948
Oval Casserole & Cover
2 qt.—10" x 7¼"

921 Leaf Shaped
Chip 'n Dip
15"x10½"

941
Individual Oval Steak Plate
11¾" x 9"

942
Divided Vegetable
10¾" x 7¼"

944
Oval Casserole & Cover
10" x 7¼" (2 pt.)

910 Bean Pot
w/cover
2 qt.

965
Dutch Oven
3 pt.

927 French Handled
Casserole w/cover
5¼"

914 Ice Jug
2 qt.

Additions to Hull's Famous Ovenproof

House 'n Garden

Serving-Ware

505 Carafe w/cover (2 cup)
506 Open Baker 32 oz.
507 Casserole w/cover 32 oz.
528 4 pc. Coffee Carafe Set

consisting of
1 only Coffee Carafe w/c
1 only Coffee Cup 7 oz.
1 only Deep Well Saucer

594 Table Size Salt Shaker
595 Table Size Pepper Shaker
596 Table Size Salt & Pepper Set

533 Fruit 6"
593 Oval Well 'n Tree Steak Plate 14" x 10"

hull pottery company
crooksville, ohio *u.s.a.*

597 Cup 7 oz.
598 Saucer 5⅞"
599 Luncheon Plate 9⅜"

Look at the angle of this. Our extra deep wells in the saucers will save many spills.

One outstanding feature also in the design is that it permits easy stacking that takes less storage area.

570 — Ovenproof 16 Piece Starter Set

4—Fruits 6"
4—Cups 7 oz.
4—Saucers 5⅞"
4—Plates 9⅜"

261

HOUSE 'n GARDEN BY HULL

OVENPROOF

Mirror Brown
Trimmed in Ivory Foam

Chicken and Duck covered one and two quart casseroles have been added to Hull's famous ovenproof House 'n Garden Servingware. Open stock House 'n Garden offers startersets, dinnersets, partypacks and many more appealing serving pieces and they are all ovenproof. The American homemaker has chosen Hull's House 'n Garden for today's casual way of life, its popularity has earned it its rightful place as the nation's number one line. It's glaze tested and meets USPA standards which conform with US Food and Drug Administration Regulations.

HULL POTTERY COMPANY • Crooksville, Ohio

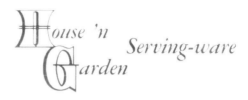

House 'n Garden *Serving-ware*

508 Oval Salad
6½" x 5¼" x 1¾"

571 Continental Mug
10 oz.

576 Custard Cup
6 oz.

573 Corn Serving Dish
9¼" x 3⅜"

583 Chip 'n Dip
11½" x 8¾"

577 Double Serving Dish
14½" x 8½"

584 Sauce Bowl
5½" Dia.

585 Tray
12" x 11"

586 Chip 'n Dip
(2 pc. Set)
Consisting of 1 each 584 and 585

512 Gravy Boat Saucer
10¼" x 6"

511 Gravy Boat
16 oz.

540 Gravy Boat Set
Consisting of 1 each 511 and 512

534 Roaster (open)
7 Pint

535 Roaster w/cover
7 Pint

557 Chicken Server
13⅜" x 10½" x 2"

508 Oval Salad
6½" x 5¼" x 1¾"

559 Server w/Chicken Cover
13⅜" L. x 10" Ht.

558 Open Chicken Baker
13⅜" x 10½" x 3"

560 Baker with Chicken Cover
13⅜" L. x 11" Ht.

575 Chicken Top, Server and Baker Set
Consisting of 556, 557, 558

hull pottery company — crooksville, ohio *u.s.a.*

House 'n Serving-ware
Garden

529 Cup 6 oz.
530 Saucer 5⅞"
531 Luncheon Plate 8½" Dia.

532 — 12 Piece Luncheon Set

4—Cups 6 oz.
4—Saucers 5⅞"
4—Luncheon Plates 8½" Dia.

536 Mixing Bowl 6
537 Mixing Bowl 7
538 Mixing Bowl — Pouring Spout 9
539—3 Pc. Mixing Bowl Set (5, 7, 9)

572 Jumbo Stein 32 oz.
574 Oval Serving Dish 10 x 6 x 1⅞
Pine Leaf Dish
591 Leaf Shaped Chip 'n Dip 12½ x 9"

592 Hen on Nest Casserole
196 Corky Piggy Bank Mirror Brown Trimmed in Blue
195 Corky Piggy Bank Mirror Brown Trimmed in Pink
194 Sitting Piggy Bank Mirror Brown Trimmed in Yellow & Turquoise
197 Jumbo Corky Piggy Bank Mirror Brown Trimmed in Yellow & Turquoise

hull pottery company — crooksville, ohio *u.s.a.*

New Addition to Hull's Famous Ovenproof

House 'n Garden *Serving-ware*

512 Gravy Boat Saucer
10¼" x 6"

511 Gravy Boat
16 oz.

540 Gravy Boat Set
Consisting of 1 each 511 and 512

587
Mushroom
Salt Shaker
3¾" Hi

588
Mushroom
Pepper Shaker
3¾" Hi

587/588 Mushroom
Salt & Pepper Set

534 Roaster (open)
7 Pint

535 Roaster w/cover
7 Pint

571 Continental Mug
10 oz.

576 Custard Cup
6 oz.

589 Bake & Serve
6½" Dia.

573 Corn Serving Dish
9¼" x 3⅜"

583 Chip 'n Dip
11½" x 8¾"

558 Open Chicken Baker
13⅜" x 10½" x 3"

575 Chicken Top, Server and Baker Set
Consisting of 556, 557, 558

557 Chicken Server
13⅜" x 10½" x 2"

559 Server w/Chicken Cover
13⅜" L. x 10" Hi

560 Baker with Chicken Cover
13⅜" L. x 11" Hi

hull pottery company -- crooksville, ohio *u.s.a.*

265

OVENPROOF **House 'n Garden** Serving-ware

NEW ITEMS 1963

567
Open French Handled
Casserole 3 pt.

562
Covered French Handled
Casserole 3 pt.

579
Covered French Handled
Casserole w Warmer

566
Pie Plate

568
Square Baker

565
Dutch Oven

569
6½" Soup & Salad Bowl

561
Covered Butter Dish

563
Ash Tray

535
Bud Vase

Hull Pottery Company, Crooksville, Ohio

for the new way of life . . .

OVENPROOF House 'n Garden Serving-ware

FOR YOUR DAILY NEEDS

| 500 Dinner Plate 10¼" Dia. | 501 Salad Plate 6½" Dia. Four Piece Place Setting | 503 Fruit 5¼" | 502 Mug 9 oz. | 522 Coffee Pot w/cover (lock lid) 60 oz. |

| 505 Mixing Bowl 5¼" | 506 Mixing Bowl 6¾" | 507 Mixing Bowl 8¼" | 509 Water Jug 5 pint | 525 Jug 2 pt. | 518 Jug ½ pt. |

| 510 Bean Pot w/cover 2 qt. | 524 Individual Bean Pot w/cover 12 oz. | 519 Sugar Bowl w/cover 4" Dia. | 518 Creamer 8 oz. | 511 Bake Dish 3 pt. 512 Casserole w/cover 3 pt. | 513 French Handled Casserole 5¼" 527 French Handled Casserole w/cover | 526 Beer Stein 16 oz. |

| 514 Ice Jug 2 qt. | 515 Salt Shaker w/cork 3¾" Hi. | 516 Pepper Shaker w/cork 3¾" Hi. | 521 Leaf Shaped Chip 'n Dip 15"X10½" | 523 Cookie Jar w/cover 94 oz. |

Mirror Brown trimmed in Ivory Foam

DISCONTINUED

541
Individual Oval Steak Plate
11¾" x 9"

542
Divided Vegetable
10¾" x 7¼"

544 Oval Casserole
w/Cover 10" x 7½" (2 pt.)

543 Oval Baker Open
10" x 7½" (2 pt.)

545—Salad or Spaghetti Bowl 10¼"
546—Three piece Salad Set consisting of:
1 only #545—Salad Bowl
1 only #547—Fork & Spoon Set

547—Fork and Spoon Set

548
Oval Casserole w/Cover
2 qt.—10" x 7½"

549
Tea Pot & Cover
5 cup

551
Jam or Mustard Jar & Cover
Set with Spoon
12 oz.

561
Covered Butter Dish
¼ lb. capacity

563
Ash Tray
8" Dia.

566
Pie Plate
9¼" Dia.

555—8 pc. Set Consisting of:
4 only #553 Soup Mugs 11 oz.
4 only #554 Trays

579 Covered French Handled
Casserole w/Warmer 3 pt.

562 Covered French Handled
Casserole 3 pt.

567 Open French Handled
Casserole 3 pt.

565 Dutch Oven 3 pt

568 Square Baker
Open 3 pt.

268

for the new way of life...

OVENPROOF **House 'n Garden** *Serving-ware*

FOR YOUR DAILY NEEDS

569
6½" Soup or Salad Bowl

500 Dinner Plate
10¼" D.a.

502 Mug
9 oz

503 Fruit
5¼"

501 Salad Plate
6½" D.a.

523 Cookie Jar
w/cover
94 oz.

578—3 PIECE PLACE SETTING

580 —3 PIECE PLACE SETTING

504 —4 PIECE PLACE SETTING

569 Water Jug
5 pint

525 Jug
2 pt

518 Jug or
Creamer
8 oz.

519 Sugar Bowl
w/cover
12 oz.

510 Bean Pot
w/cover
2 qt

524 Individual Bean
Pot w/cover
12 oz.

522 Coffee Pot
w/cover
8 cup

527 French Handled
Casserole — Cover 9¼

513 French Handled
Casserole Open

514 Ice Jug
2 qt

515 Salt Shaker
w/cork
3¾" Hi.

516 Pepper Shaker
w/cork
3¾" Hi.

521 Leaf Shaped
Chip 'n Dip
15" x 10½

516 Beer Stein
16 oz

hull pottery company — crooksville, ohio *u.s.a.*

269

House 'n Garden Serving-ware by Hull

526—16 oz.
Beer Stein

571—10 oz.
Continental Mug

592
Hen on Nest Casserole

5280—2 Pt.
Casserole w/Duck Cover

5770—2 Qt.
Casserole w/Duck Cover

5850—2 Qt.
Casserole w/Chicken Cover

5840—2 Pt.
Casserole w/Chicken Cover

542—10¾" x 7¼"
Divided Vegetable

540 Gravy Boat Set
Consisting of 1 each 511 and 512

196 Sitting
Piggy Bank

195 Corky
Piggy Bank

197 Jumbo Corky
Piggy Bank

545—10½" Salad
or Spaghetti Bowl

547—Fork and Spoon Set
546—3 Piece Salad Set Consisting of:
1 only #545—Salad Bowl
1 only #547—Fork and Spoon Set

593—14" x 10"
Oval Well 'n Tree
Steak Plate

541—11¾" x 9"
Ind. Oval Steak Plate

565—3 Pt. Dutch Oven
Consists of two only
568—3 Pt. Square Baker

544—10" x 7¼" (2 Pt.)
Oval Casserole
w/Cover
543—10" x 7¼" (2 Pt.)
Oval Baker Open

548—10" x 7¼" (2 Qt.)
Oval Casserole

THE UNITED STATES
GLAZE TESTED
APPROVED
POTTERS ASSOCIATION

270

Mirror Brown trimmed in Ivory Foam

514—2 Qt.
Ice Jug

525—2 Pt.
Jug

509—5 Pt.
Jug

522—8 Cup
Coffee Pot

507—32 oz.
Casserole w/Cover
506—32 oz. Casserole Open

536—6"
Mixing Bowl

537—7"
Mixing Bowl

538—8"
Mixing Bowl
w/Pouring Spout

539—3 Pc. Mixing Bowl Set
(6", 7", 8")

579—3 Pt. Covered French
Handled Casserole w/Warmer

562—3 Pt. Covered French
Handled Casserole
567—3 Pt. Open French
Handled Casserole

527—5¼"
French Handled Casserole
with Cover
513 French Handled
Casserole Open

521—15" x 10½"
Leaf Shaped
Chip 'n Dip

563—8" Dia.
Ash Tray

549—5 Cup
Tea Pot

hull pottery company—crooksville, ohio *u.s.a.*

271

for the new way of life. . .
OVENPROOF House 'n Garden Serving-ware
FOR YOUR DAILY USE
THE UNITED STATES POTTERS ASSOCIATION
GLAZE TESTED APPROVED
569—6½" Soup or Salad Bowl
500—10¼" Dia. Dinner Plate
502—9 oz. Mug
503—5¼" Fruit
501—6½" Dia. Salad Plate
523—94 oz. Cookie Jar
578—3 Piece Place Setting
580—3 Piece Place Setting
504—4 Piece Place Setting
531—8½" Dia. Luncheon Plate
529—6 oz. Cup
530—5½" Saucer
533—6" Fruit
599—9⅜" Luncheon Plate
597—7 oz. Cup
598—5⅞" Saucer
510—2 Qt. Bean Pot
532—12 Piece Luncheon Set
570—Starter Set
515—3¾" Hi Salt Shaker w/Cork
516—3¾" Hi Pepper Shaker w/Cork
587—3¾" Hi 588—3¾" Hi Mushroom Salt and Pepper Shaker
519—12 oz. Sugar Bowl
518—8 oz. Jug or Creamer
561—¼ lb. Covered Butter Dish
524—12 oz. Ind. Bean Pot
551—12 oz. Jam or Mustard Jar and Cover Set with Spoon
576—6 oz. Custard Cup
566—9¼" Pie Plate
555—8 pc. Set Consisting of: 4 only #553 Soup Mugs 11 oz. 4 only #554 Trays
589—6½" Dia. Bake & Serve
574—10" x 5" x 1⅝" Hi Oval Serving Dish

hull pottery company–crooksville, ohio *u.s.a.*

Dept. 23

CLASSIFICATION 1

B.M.S. L-O
BDJV-1-2-3

Mirror Brown trimmed in Ivory Foam

for the new way of life...

OVENPROOF **H**ouse 'n **G**arden Serving-ware

FOR YOUR DAILY NEEDS

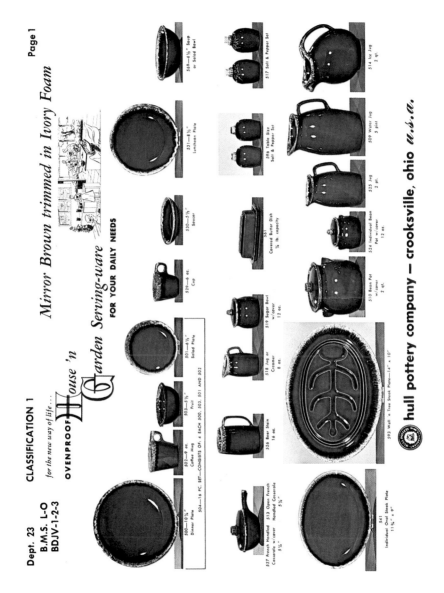

500—10½"
Dinner Plate

501—9 oz.
Coffee Mug

503—5½"
Fruit

501—6½"
Salad Plate

504—16 PC. SET—CONSISTS OF: 4 EACH 500, 503, 501 AND 502

531—8½"
Luncheon Plate

530—5½"
Saucer

529—oz.
Cup

569—6½" Soup
or Salad Bowl

517 Salt & Pepper Set

599 Table Size
Salt & Pepper Set

561
Covered Butter Dish
¼ lb. capacity

519 Sugar Bowl
12 oz.

518 Jug or
Creamer
8 oz.

526 Beer Stein
16 oz.

527 French Handled 513 Open French
Casserole w/cover Handled Casserole
5¼"   5¼"

541
Individual Oval Steak Plate
11¾" x 9"

593 Well n Tree Steak Plate—14" x 10"

510 Bean Pot
w/cover
2 qt.

524 Individual Bean
Pot w/cover
12 oz.

525 Jug
2 pt.

509 Water Jug
5 pint

514 Ice Jug
2 qt.

hull pottery company — crooksville, ohio *u.s.a.*

273

RAINBOW
BY HULL

#260—12 Piece Rainbow Dinnerware Set
consisting of:
4 only 10½" Plates
4 only 9 oz. Mugs
4 only Soup & Salad Bowls—6½"

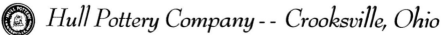

Hull Pottery Company -- Crooksville, Ohio

OVENPROOF RAINBOW LUNCHEON SET

by Hull

#232—12 pc.
Plate 8½"
Cup 6 oz.
Saucer 5½"

LUNCHEON SET
Illustrated

Mirror Brown   Butterscotch   Green Agate   Tangerine

Complete set also available in choice of each color shown—see list.

Also available in the four colors shown above.

No. 590 Individual
Leaf Dish 7¼" x 4¾"

No. 591 Leaf Shape
Chip 'n Dip 12¼" x 9"

Discontinued

Here is a new Mixing Bowl Set added
to Hull's Famous line of House 'n Garden
Serving and Kitchen Ware

No. 539—3 pc.
Mixing Bowl Set
(6"—7"—8")
Mirror Brown only

No. 538 Mixing
Bowl w/Pouring
Spout 8"

No. 537
Mixing Bowl 7"

No. 536
Mixing Bowl 6"

Mixing Bowls and Serv-all Trays sold only
in Mirror Brown.

Discontinued

The complete line of House 'n Garden is available in Mirror
Brown trimmed in Ivory Foam . . . See list for other items also
offered in "Rainbow" assorted colors.

hull pottery company — crooksville, ohio *u.s.a.*

Classification 1

935
Bud Vase
9" Ht.

941
Individual Oval Steak Plate
11¾" x 9"

948
Oval Casserole & Cover
2 qt—10" x 7¼"

949
Tea Pot & Cover
5 cup

966
Pie Plate
9¼" Dia.

942
Divided Vegetable
10¾" x 7¼"

944
Oval Casserole & Cover
10" x 7¼" (2 pt.)
943 Open Oval Baker

951
Jam or Mustard Jar & Cover
Set with Spoon
12 oz.

955—8 pc. Set Consisting of:
4 only # 953 Soup Mugs 11 oz.
4 only # 954 Trays

979
Covered French Handled
Casserole w/Warmer
3 pt.
962 French Handled Casserole & Cover
967 Open French Handled Casserole

945—Salad or Spaghetti Bowl 10½"
946—Three piece Salad Set consisting of:
1 only #945—Salad Bowl
1 only #947—Fork & Spoon Set

947—Fork and Spoon Set

963
Ash Tray
8" Dia.

961
Covered Butter Dish
¼ lb. capacity

RAINBOW

202
Coffee Set of 4 Rainbow

9 oz.
201—9 oz. Coffee Mugs in
Rainbow Colors

965
Dutch Oven
3 pt.

Hull Pottery Company
Crooksville, Ohio

990
Ind. Leaf Server
5" x 7½"

991
Chip 'N Dip Server
9½" x 12"

276

Classification 1

DEPT. 23 BMSL-DIV 1-2-3

for the new way of life...

OVENPROOF House 'n Garden Serving-ware

FOR YOUR DAILY NEEDS

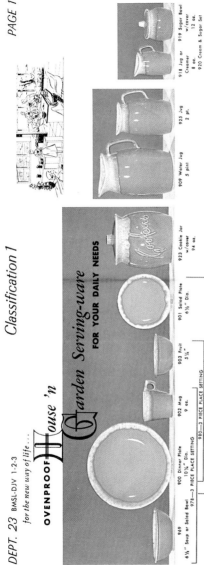

969
6½" Soup or Salad Bowl
978—3 PIECE PLACE SETTING

900 Dinner Plate
10¼" Dia.
980—3 PIECE PLACE SETTING

902 Mug
9 oz.
904—4 PIECE PLACE SETTING

903 Fruit
5¼"

901 Salad Plate
6½" Dia.

923 Cookie Jar
w/cover
94 oz.

909 Water Jug
5 pint

925 Jug
2 pt.

918 Jug or Creamer
8 oz.

919 Sugar Bowl
w/cover
12 oz.

920 Cream & Sugar Set

The famous mirror brown House 'n Garden serving-ware now also available in tangerine -- identified as 900 Series -- all Oven Proof

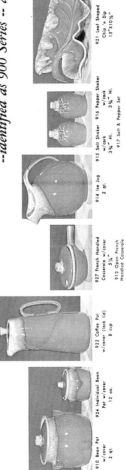

910 Bean Pot
w/cover
2 qt.

924 Individual Bean Pot w/cover
12 oz.

922 Coffee Pot
w/cover (lock lid)
8 cup

927 French Handled Casserole w/cover
5½"
913 Open French Handled Casserole

914 Ice Jug
2 qt.

915 Salt Shaker
w/cork
3¾" Hi.

916 Pepper Shaker
w/cork   3¾" Hi.

917 Salt & Pepper Set

921 Leaf Shaped Chip 'n Dip
15"X10½"

926 Beer Stein
16 oz.

Hull Pottery Company, Crooksville, Ohio

277

House 'n Garden Serving-ware

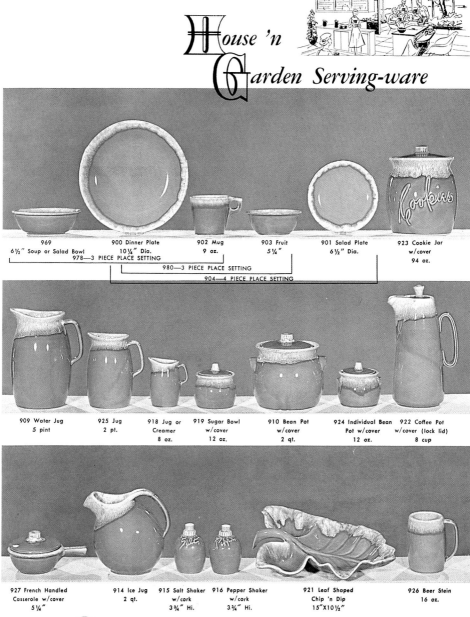

969 6½" Soup or Salad Bowl	900 Dinner Plate 10¼" Dia.	902 Mug 9 oz.	903 Fruit 5¼"	901 Salad Plate 6½" Dia.	923 Cookie Jar w/cover 94 oz.

978—3 PIECE PLACE SETTING

980—3 PIECE PLACE SETTING

904—4 PIECE PLACE SETTING

909 Water Jug 5 pint	925 Jug 2 pt.	918 Jug or Creamer 8 oz.	919 Sugar Bowl w/cover 12 oz.	910 Bean Pot w/cover 2 qt.	924 Individual Bean Pot w/cover 12 oz.	922 Coffee Pot w/cover (lock lid) 8 cup

927 French Handled Casserole w/cover 5¼"	914 Ice Jug 2 qt.	915 Salt Shaker w/cork 3¾" Hi.	916 Pepper Shaker w/cork 3¾" Hi.	921 Leaf Shaped Chip 'n Dip 15"X10½"	926 Beer Stein 16 oz.

Hull Pottery Company, Crooksville, Ohio

278

The famous mirror brown House 'n Garden serving-ware now also available in tangerine --identified as 900 Series -- all Oven Proof

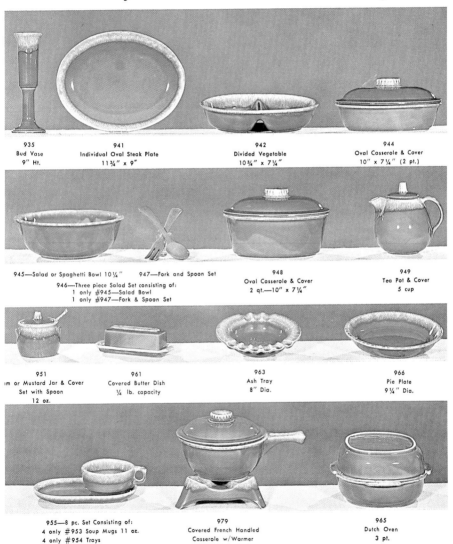

935
Bud Vase
9" Ht.

941
Individual Oval Steak Plate
11¾" x 9"

942
Divided Vegetable
10¾" x 7¼"

944
Oval Casserole & Cover
10" x 7¼" (2 pt.)

945—Salad or Spaghetti Bowl 10¼"
946—Three piece Salad Set consisting of:
1 only #945—Salad Bowl
1 only #947—Fork & Spoon Set

947—Fork and Spoon Set

948
Oval Casserole & Cover
2 qt.—10" x 7¼"

949
Tea Pot & Cover
5 cup

951
am or Mustard Jar & Cover
Set with Spoon
12 oz.

961
Covered Butter Dish
¼ lb. capacity

963
Ash Tray
8" Dia.

966
Pie Plate
9¼" Dia.

955—8 pc. Set Consisting of:
4 only #953 Soup Mugs 11 oz.
4 only #954 Trays

979
Covered French Handled
Casserole w/Warmer
3 pt.

965
Dutch Oven
3 pt.

Country Squire SERVING-WARE

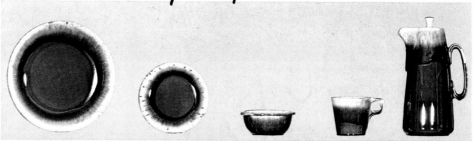

| 100 Dinner Plate 10¼" Dia. | 101 Salad Plate 6½" Dia. | 103 Fruit 5¼" | 102 Mug 9 oz. | 122 Coffee Pot w/cover (lock lid) 60 oz. |

⌊————————— Four Piece Place Setting —————————⌋

| 105 Mixing Bowl 5¼" | 106 Mixing Bowl 6¾" | 107 Mixing Bowl 8¼" | 109 Water Jug 5 pint | 125 Jug 2 pt. | 118 Jug ½ pt. |

| 110 Bean Pot w/cover 2 qt. | 124 Individual Bean Pot w/cover 12 oz. | 119 Sugar Bowl w/cover 4" Dia. | 118 Creamer 8 oz. | 111 Bake Dish 3 pt. 112 Casserole w/cover 3 pt. | 113 French Handled Casserole 5¼" 127 French Handled Casserole w/cover | 126 Beer Stein 16 oz. |

| 114 Ice Jug 2 qt. | 115 Salt Shaker w/cork 3¾" Hi. | 116 Pepper Shaker w/cork 3¾" Hi. | 121 Leaf Shaped Chip 'n Dip 15"X10½" | 123 Cookie Jar w/cover 94 oz. |

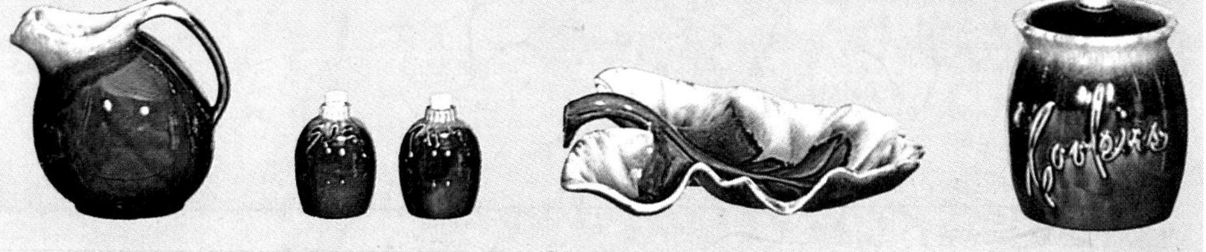

280

145
Salad or Spaghetti Bowl
10¼"

121 Leaf Shaped
Chip 'n Dip
15" x 10½"

166
Pie Plate

125 Jug
2 pt.

114 Ice Jug
2 qt.

149
Tea Pot & Cover
5 cup

122 Coffee Pot
w/cover (lock lid)
60 oz.

127 Salt & Pepper Set

161
Covered Butter Dish

124 Individual Bean
Pot w/cover
12 oz.

123 Cookie Jar
w/cover
94 oz.

120 Sugar & Creamer Set

151
Jam or Mustard Jar & Cover
Set with Spoon
12 oz.

126 Beer Stein
16 oz.

#155—8 pc. Set Consisting of:
4 only #153 Soup Mugs 11 oz.
4 only #154 Trays

#156—8 pc. Set Consisting of:
4 only #102 Coffee Mugs 9 oz.
4 only #154 Trays

164
Ceramic Warmer
with Candle

163
Ash Tray

135
Bud Vase

Hull Pottery Company, Crooksville, Ohio

Crestone ©
hull u.s.a.
OVEN-PROOF

an ovenproof creation

300 Dinner Plate
10¼"

301 Salad
or Dessert Plate
7½"

302 Coffee Mug
9 oz.

303 Fruit
6"

304 Bread
and Butter Plate
6½"

305 Carafé
w/Cover
(2 Cup)

306 Open Baker
32 oz.

307 Casserole
w/Cover
32 oz.

308 Indiv. Casserole
w/Cover
9 oz.

310 Gravy Boat
or Syrup
10 oz.

·311 Saucer For
Gravy Boat or Syrup
6½"

313 French Handled
Casserole
9 oz.

312 Two Piece Gravy Boat Set

hull pottery company —
crooksville, ohio u.s.a.

314 Custard Cup
6 oz.

315 Salt Shaker
3¾"
316 Pepper Shaker
3¾"
317 Salt and Pepper Set

318 Creamer
8 oz.

319 Sugar Bowl
w/Cover
8 oz.
320 Sugar and Creamer Set

321 Chip 'n Dip Leaf
14¼"x10¼"x2¼"

322 Coffee Server
w/Cover
(8 Cup)

for casual living ---

| 325 Beverage Pitcher 38 oz. | 326 Party Beverage Stein 14 oz. | 327 French Hdld. Casserole w/Cover 9 oz. | 329 Cup 7 oz. | 330 Saucer 5 7/8" | 331 Luncheon Plate 9 3/8" |

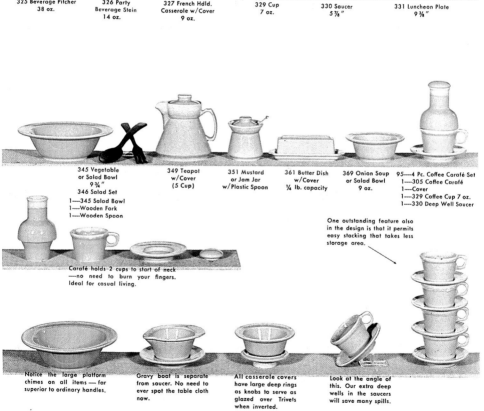

345 Vegetable or Salad Bowl 9 3/4"
346 Salad Set
1—345 Salad Bowl
1—Wooden Fork
1—Wooden Spoon

349 Teapot w/Cover (5 Cup)

351 Mustard or Jam Jar w/Plastic Spoon

361 Butter Dish w/Cover 1/4 lb. capacity

369 Onion Soup or Salad Bowl 9 oz.

95—4 Pc. Coffee Carafé Set
1—305 Coffee Carafé
1—Cover
1—329 Coffee Cup 7 oz.
1—330 Deep Well Saucer

One outstanding feature also in the design is that it permits easy stacking that takes less storage area.

Carafé holds 2 cups to start of neck —no need to burn your fingers. Ideal for casual living.

Notice the large platform chimes on all items — far superior to ordinary handles.

Gravy boat is separate from saucer. No need to ever spot the table cloth now.

All casserole covers have large deep rings as knobs to serve as glazed over Trivets when inverted.

Look at the angle of this. Our extra deep wells in the saucers will save many spills.

for the new way of life . . .

OVENPROOF House 'n Garden Serving-ware

FOR YOUR DAILY NEEDS

669
6½" Soup/Salad

600 Dinner Plate
10¼" Dia.

602 Mug
9 oz.

603 Fruit
5¼"

601 Salad Plate
6½"

604—4 PIECE PLACE SETTING

615 Salt Shaker
w/cork 3¾" Hi.

616 Pepper Shaker
w/cork 3¾" Hi.

618
Creamer 8 oz.

619 Sugar Bowl
w/Cover 12 oz.

627 Fr. Handled Casserole
w/Cover 12 oz.

633 Fruit
6"

626 Beer Stein
16 oz.

617 Salt & Pepper Set   620 Sugar & Creamer Set

622 Coffee Pot
w/Cover 8 Cup

649 Tea Pot
w/Cover 5 Cup

625 Jug
2 pt.

621 Chip 'n Dip

641 Oval Steak Plate
11¾" x 9"

642 Divided Vegetable Dish
10¾" x 7¼"

648 Deep Oval Casserole
w/Cover 2 qt.

hull pottery company — crooksville, ohio *u.s.a.*

284

AVOCADO *with Ivory trim*

| 666 Pie Plate 9 ¼ " Dia. | 624 Ind. Bean Pot w/Cover 12 oz. | 610 Bean Pot w/Cover 2 qt. | 699 Luncheon Plate 9 ⅜ " Dia. |

| 698 Saucer 5 ⅜ " | 697 Cup 7 oz. | 651 Jam or Mustard Jar w/Cover Set w/Spoon 12 oz. | 661 Covered Butter Dish (¼ lb. Capacity) | 674 Oval Bake 'n Serve Dish 10" x 5" x 1 ⅜ " |

624-4 Beer Stein 16 oz.
4 Piece Party Pack Set
(Individual Carton 6 Sets to Master)

604—Oven Proof 16 Piece Starter Set

| 4 - Fruits—5 ¼ " | 4 - Salad Plates—6 ½ " |
| 4 - Mugs—9 oz. | 4 - Dinner Plates—10 ¼ " Dia. |

670—Oven Proof 16 Piece Starter Set

| 4 - Fruits—6" | 4 - Saucers—5 ⅞ " |
| 4 - Cups—7 oz. | 4 - Luncheon Plates—9 ⅜ " Dia. |

Mirror Brown trimmed in Ivory Foam

Additions to the nation's #1 line for casual living

House 'n Garden Serving-ware

591—9¼"

595
11½" × 7¾" × 1¾"

594
6¾" × 4¾"

596
11¼" × 7½"

Canisters

556
5½" × 5½"

557
6¼" × 6¼"

The nation's number one line for casual living offers these new creations.

This newly designed canister set is available in four sizes.

The flour and sugar canisters each have a liberal capacity of five pounds, the most commonly purchased package size. Since coffee and tea are available, either bulk or packaged, capacity is not indicated.

No homemaker's kitchen is complete without the spoon rest and the handled serving dish.

Much thought has been given to every detail and purpose of the **individual** fish platter and handled serving dish.

Our deviled egg server takes less space on your table yet holds one/half dozen eggs. You will never worry about them rolling off with our specially shaped wells.

558
7¼" × 8"

559
9" × 9¼"

hull pottery company–crooksville, ohio *u.s.a.*

Mirror Brown trimmed in Ivory Foam

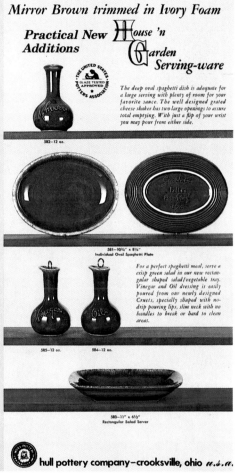
287

for the new way of life . . .

OVENPROOF

House 'n Garden Serving-ware

FOR YOUR DAILY USE

800 — 10¼" Dia. Dinner Plate

801 — 6½" Dia. Salad Plate

802 — 9 Oz. Mug

803 — 5¼" Fruit

804 — 16 Pc. Set

808 — 4 Pc. Place Setting

MIRROR ALMOND WITH CARAMEL TRIM

818 — 10 Oz. Creamer

819 — 12 Oz. Sugar Bowl w/cover

841 — 11¾" × 9" Ind. Oval Steak Plate

867 — 11" × 8¾" Handled Vegetable Server

820 — Sugar & Creamer Set

828 — Completer Set

813 — 12 Oz. Open French Handled Casserole

827 — 12 Oz. Covered French Handled Casserole

887 — 3¾" Hi. Mushroom Salt Shaker

888 — 3¾" Hi. Mushroom Pepper Shaker

887/888 — Mushroom Salt & Pepper Set

826 — 16 Oz. Beer Stein

842 — 10¾" × 7¼" Divided Vegetable

873 — 8¾" × 4" Small Oval Serving Dish

500 ALC — 2½ Oz. Ramekin

hull pottery company - crooksville, ohio 43731 *u.s.a*

2/81

for the new way of life . . .

OVENPROOF

House 'n Garden Serving-ware

FOR YOUR DAILY USE

836 — 6"
Mixing Bowl

837 — 7"
Mixing Bowl

838 — 8"
Mixing Bowl

839 — 3 Pc. Mixing Bowl Set (1 each #836-837-838)

MIRROR ALMOND WITH CARAMEL TRIM

869 — 6½"
Soup or Salad Bowl

853 — 11 Oz.
Soup Mug

854 — 9½" x 5¾"
Tray

855 — 8 Pc. Soup 'n Sandwich Set (4 each #853-854)

hull pottery company

- crooksville, ohio 43731 *u.s.a.*

289

Walnut Ridge

12 pc. Set
4 ea. Dinner Plate, Bowl, Mug

16 pc. Set
4 ea. Dinner Plate, Salad Plate, Bowl, Mug

20 pc. Set
4 ea. Dinner Plate, Salad Plate, Bowl, Cup, Saucer

Completer Set
1 ea. Sugar w/Cover, Creamer, Vegetable Bowl, Steak Plate

6 pc. Snack Set
2 ea. Tray, Bowl, Mug

Sugar & Creamer Set

Salt & Pepper Set

See price list for open stock.

Flint Ridge

12 pc. Set
4 ea. Dinner Plate, Bowl, Mug

16 pc. Set
4 ea. Dinner Plate, Salad Plate, Bowl, Mug

20 pc. Set
4 ea. Dinner Plate, Salad Plate, Bowl, Cup, Saucer

Completer Set
1 ea. Sugar w/Cover, Creamer, Vegetable Bowl, Steak Plate

6 pc. Snack Set
2 ea. Tray, Bowl, Mug

Sugar & Creamer Set

Salt & Pepper Set

Tawny Ridge

12 pc. Set
4 ea. Dinner Plate, Bowl, Mug

16 pc. Set
4 ea. Dinner Plate, Salad Plate, Bowl, Mug

20 pc. Set
4 ea. Dinner Plate, Salad Plate, Bowl, Cup, Saucer

Completer Set
1 ea. Sugar w/Cover, Creamer, Vegetable Bowl, Steak Plate

6 pc. Snack Set
2 ea. Tray, Bowl, Mug

Sugar & Creamer Set

Salt & Pepper Set

**64 OZ. COFFEE
SERVER W/COVER**
1522 GRAY
2522 SAND
522 BROWN

**80 OZ. WATER
JUG**
1509 GRAY
2509 SAND
509 BROWN

72 OZ. ICE JUG
1514 GRAY
2514 SAND
514 BROWN

**32 OZ.
CASSEROLE
W/COVER**
1507 GRAY
2507 SAND
507 BROWN

**80 OZ. BEAN POT
W/COVER**
1510 GRAY
2510 SAND
510 BROWN

10 OZ. MUG
102 GRAY
202 SAND
302 BROWN

12 OZ. FRUIT
503 BROWN

SALAD PLATE, 6½"
501 BROWN

10 OZ. CREAMER
1518 GRAY
2518 SAND
518 BROWN

**DINNER PLATE,
10¼"**
500 BROWN

STARTER SET
504 BROWN
4-10¼" DINNER PLATES
4-6½" SALAD PLATES
4-10 OZ. MUGS
4-12 OZ. FRUITS

293

96 OZ. COOKIE JAR W/COVER
1523 GRAY
2523 SAND
523 BROWN

36 OZ. JUG
1525 GRAY
2525 SAND
525 BROWN

3 PC. MIXING BOWL SET, (6"-7"-8")
1539 GRAY
2539 SAND
539 BROWN

60 OZ. MIXING BOWL W/POURING SPOUT, 8"
1538 GRAY
2538 SAND
538 BROWN

21 OZ. MIXING BOWL, 6"
1536 GRAY
2536 SAND
536 BROWN

40 OZ. MIXING BOWL, 7"
1537 GRAY
2537 SAND
537 BROWN

18 OZ. STEIN
1526 GRAY
2526 SAND
526 BROWN

12 OZ. ONION SOUP W/COVER
1535 GRAY
2535 SAND
535 BROWN

12 OZ. ONION SOUP
1534 GRAY
2534 SAND
534 BROWN

INDIVIDUAL OVAL STEAK PLATE
541 BROWN

13 OZ. INDIVIDUAL BEAN POT W/COVER
1524 GRAY
2524 SAND
524 BROWN

12 OZ. FRENCH HANDLED CASSEROLE
1513 GRAY
2513 SAND
513 BROWN

12 OZ. FRENCH HANDLED CASSEROLE W/COVER
1527 GRAY
2527 SAND
527 BROWN

294

68 OZ. DEEP OVAL CASSEROLE W/COVER
1548 GRAY
2548 SAND
548 BROWN

90 OZ. SALAD OR SPAGHETTI BOWL, 10¼"
1545 GRAY
2545 SAND
545 BROWN

40 OZ. TEA POT AND COVER
1549 GRAY
2549 SAND
549 BROWN

38 OZ. OVAL CASSEROLE W/COVER
1544 GRAY
2644 SAND
544 BROWN

14 OZ. SOUP MUG
1553 GRAY
2553 SAND
553 BROWN

TRAY, 9½" x 5¾"
1554 GRAY
2564 SAND
554 BROWN

BUTTER DISH W/COVER
1561 GRAY
2561 SAND
561 BROWN

13 OZ. JAM OR MUSTARD JAR W/COVER
1550 GRAY
2550 SAND
550 BROWN

12 OZ.
CONTINENTAL
MUG
1571 GRAY
2571 SAND
571 BROWN

21 OZ. SOUP OR
SALAD BOWL
1569 GRAY
2569 SAND
569 BROWN

50 OZ. SQUARE
BAKER
1568 GRAY
2568 SAND
568 BROWN

PIE PLATE, 9¼"
1566 GRAY
2566 SAND
566 BROWN

34 OZ.
INDIVIDUAL
OVAL
SPAGHETTI
PLATE
1581 GRAY
2581 SAND
581 BROWN

OVAL WELL 'N
TREE STEAK
PLATE
593 BROWN

9 OZ. FRENCH
HANDLED
CASSEROLE
W/COVER
579 BROWN

OZ. FRENCH
HANDLED
CASSEROLE
562 BROWN

16 OZ. OVAL
SERVING DISH
1574 GRAY
2574 SAND
574 BROWN

9½ OZ. SMALL
OVAL SERVING
DISH
1573 GRAY
2573 SAND
573 BROWN

BAKE &
SERVE, 6½"
1589 GRAY
2589 SAND
589 BROWN

8 OZ. CUSTARD
CUP
176 GRAY
276 SAND
376 BROWN

MUSHROOM
SALT & PEPPER
SET
587/588 BROWN

2½ OZ. RAMEKIN
1600 GRAY
2600 SAND
600 BROWN

4 PC. CANISTER SET
160 GRAY
260 SAND
360 BROWN

GINGERBREAD MAN COOKIE JAR
123 GRAY
223 SAND
323 BROWN

38 OZ. CASSEROLE W/DUCK COVER
15280 GRAY
25280 SAND
5280 BROWN

68 OZ. CASSEROLE W/CHICKEN COVER
15850 GRAY
25850 SAND
5850 BROWN

SITTING PIGGY BANK
1196 GRAY
2196 SAND
196 BROWN

32 OZ. CASSEROLE W/COVER
114 GRAY
214 SAND
314 BROWN

CORKY PIGGY BANK
1195 GRAY
2195 SAND
195 BROWN

18 OZ. SERVER W/HANDLE
1595 GRAY
2595 SAND
595 BROWN

13 OZ. GARLIC CELLAR
1505 GRAY
2505 SAND
3505 BROWN

GINGERBREAD BOY COASTER/ SPOON REST,
5" x 5"
199 GRAY
299 SAND
399 BROWN

GINGERBREAD MAN SERVER, 10" x 10"
1198 GRAY
2198 SAND
198 BROWN

297

539
3 Pc.
Mixing Bowl
Set (6-7-8")

5439 — Consists of 1 each: **5436, 5438, 5440**

5414 5 Piece Place Setting
Consists of 1 each:
5400, 5401, 5402, 5403, 5404

5435 Completer Set
Consists of 1 each:
5408, 5441, 5452

5404 16 Piece Set
Consists of 4 each:
5400, 5401, 5402, 5403

504 Starter Set
Consists of 4 each:
500, 501, 503, 302

504 Starter Set
Consists of 4 each:
500 Dinner Plate 10¼"
501 Salad Plae 6½"
502 Fruit 5¼"
302 Mug 10 oz.

5414 5 Pc. Place Setting consists of 1 each: 5400, 5401, 5402, 5403, 5404

5470 - 36 oz. Pitcher   **5472** - 66 oz. Pitcher

5435 Completer Set consists of 1 each: 5408, 5441, 5452

504 16 Pc. Starter - Consists of 1 each: 500, 501, 302, 503

327 AMERINE STREET
CROOKSVILLE, OHIO 43731
614/982-2075   614/982-2085

436 6" Bowl   **438** 8" Bowl   **440** 10" Bowl

404 16 Piece Place Setting
Consists of 4 each:
400, 401, 402, 403

406 4 Piece Place Setting
Consists of 1 each:
400, 401, 402, 403

414 5 Piece Place Setting
Consists of 1 each:
400, 401, 402, 403, 405

420 20 Piece Place Setting
Consists of 4 each:
400, 401, 402, 403, 405

414 5 Piece Place Setting

474 Pitcher & Bowl Set

435 Completer Set

452 Sugar & Creamer Set

435 Completer Set   Consists of 1 each: 408, 441, 452

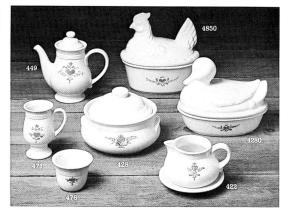

327 AMERINE STREET
CROOKSVILLE, OHIO 43731

HULL POTTERY CROOKSVILLE OHIO

6440
6436
6470
6438
65280
6517
6472
6595
6568
6444
6410
6490
6428
6453
6423
6567
65850
6472
6473
6474

303

6441

71

6408

6403

6402

6422

6452

6476

6405

6401

6400

6423

6419

6471

6418

6462

6442

6425

6449

304

Index